POISONED LEGACY

POISONED LEGACY

The Decline and Fall of the
Nineteenth Egyptian Dynasty

Aidan Dodson

The American University in Cairo Press
Cairo   New York

This paperback edition published in 2016 by
The American University in Cairo Press
113 Sharia Kasr el Aini, Cairo, Egypt
420 Fifth Avenue, New York, NY 10018
www.aucpress.com

Dar el Kutub No. 14338/15
ISBN 978 977 416 752 2

Dar el Kutub Cataloging-in-Publication Data

Dodson, Aidan
       Poisoned Legacy: The Fall of the 19th Egyptian Dynasty: Revised Edition / Aidan Dodson.—
Cairo: The American University in Cairo Press, 2016.
       p. cm.
       ISBN 978 977 416 752 2
       1. Egypt—Antiquities
       932

1 2 3 4 5   20 19 18 17 16

Designed by Adam El Sehemy
Printed in Egypt

To the memories of
William Joseph Murnane (1945–2000)
and
Francis Joseph Yurco (1944–2004)

CONTENTS

ILLUSTRATIONS

All images are by the author except where otherwise stated.

PREFACE

The later years of the Nineteenth Dynasty have received relatively little attention from Egyptologists. The reasons for this derive not only from their position between the relatively well-documented reigns of Rameses II and Rameses III, but also from the myriad uncertainties surrounding the era—even the succession of kings remains debated to this day. However, it is these very uncertainties that make the period a fertile ground for research, and first attracted me to it.

Like the notorious Amarna Period of a century and a half earlier, a feature of the period is the way in which Egyptian posterity attempted to erase a number of its protagonists from the historical record. Similarly, events of potentially crucial import are hinted at only by fragmentary and/or equivocal data, meaning that there are perhaps as many interpretations of what might have occurred as there are scholars who have seriously studied the period.

Accordingly, any attempt at producing a single account of the years between the death of Rameses II and the accession of Rameses III can in no way present a "consensus" view, as such a thing does not at present exist! However, while putting forward what I believe to be—on the present evidence, at least—the most plausible reconstruction of events, I have also tried as far as possible to note where others' opinions differ from mine, and in any case lay out the range of evidence on which any view of any episode has to be based.

This book is dedicated to the memory of two scholars whose contributions to the history of the Nineteenth Dynasty were immense, and whose premature demise has left Egyptology poorer. Some of the conclusions reached here differ from those obtained by Bill Murnane and Frank Yurco—in particular as regards the ancestry, and nature of the reign, of Amenmeses, about which Frank and I published a pair of papers with diametrically opposite conclusions in the 1997 issue of the *Journal of the American Research Center in Egypt*. However, without their work on the monuments of the period, in particular at Karnak, much of this still opaque era would have remained even more obscure. Bill was particularly generous in sharing his data, and my wife Dyan and I cherish the memory of a final Chinese meal with him in Luxor, only a few months before his untimely death.

My work also owes much, of course, to the work of a whole range of other scholars, in particular that carried out on the reign of Amenmeses by Rolf Krauss, and the heroic documentation of the Ramesside Period by Kenneth Kitchen, without which any work on that era would be immeasurably more laborious. The work of Otto Schaden in the tomb of Amenmeses should also be highlighted as producing the sort of fresh data that are crucial if any of the suppositions that underlie so much of Egyptian historical research are to be replaced by newer ones built upon firmer foundations. Similarly, Peter Brand's continuation of Bill Murnane's epigraphic labors at Karnak is once again allowing scholars access to the facts on the ground (or, rather, wall) to replace less rigorous reports of the past. However, the work of our predecessors remains of importance, particularly where the evidence they recorded no longer exists: witness the bombing of Liverpool Museum in 1941 that resulted in the loss of two of the already rare monuments of Amenmeses, one of which held crucial, if ambiguous, evidence that can now only be assessed via the notes of Percy Newberry, Eric Peet, and Bryan Emery (see p. 32, below).

Various other friends and colleagues are also owed my thanks for all kinds of help over the years during which I have worked on this period and on this book, including Catherine Bridonneau; Ashley Cooke; Tom Hardwick; Salima Ikram; Ray Johnson and his colleagues at Chicago House, Luxor; Jaromir Malek; Sara Orel; Bob Partridge; Catherine Rohrig; Otto Schaden; and Jürgen Schesser. As always, I am indebted to my wife, Dyan Hilton, for all her support, and to her, Martin Davies, Reg Clark, and Sheila Hilton for reading and commenting on the manuscript; I am also indebted to Martin for allowing me to freely plunder his photographic collection and use so many choice items from it. In conclusion, however, I remain wholly to blame for all errors and questionable statements that remain within the covers of this book.

September 2009

As is the usual case in Egyptian archaeology, where research continues apace across a wide front, a number of new publications relevant to the topic of this book have appeared since its first publication five years ago, including some that make substantive changes to the interpretation of data upon which it is based. Accordingly, the appearance of this paper-covered edition has been used as an opportunity to update the text and bibliography in a number of areas.

Department of Archaeology and Anthropology   May 2015
University of Bristol

ABBREVIATIONS
AND
CONVENTIONS

Berlin	Ägyptisches Museum und Papyrussamlung, Berlin.
BM	British Museum, London.
BMA	Brooklyn Museum of Art.
Cairo	Egyptian Museum, Cairo.
exc.	excavation number.
IFAO	Cairo, Institut français d'Archéologie orientale
l.p.h.	life, prosperity, health (𓋹𓍑𓋴, ꜥnḫ wḏꜣ snb), the wish often appended to the name of the king in inscriptions.
MFA	Museum of Fine Arts, Boston.
MMA	Metropolitan Museum of Art, New York.
o	ostracon (followed by current location/number).
p	papyrus (followed by current location/number).
Petrie	Petrie Museum, University College London.
RMO	Rijksmuseum van Oudheden, Leiden.
TT	Theban Tomb.
UPMAA	University of Pennsylvania Museum of Archaeology and Anthropology, Philadelphia.

Where titles of individuals are capitalized, they are more or less direct translations of the original Egyptian. Renderings of Egyptian names are intended as far as possible to preserve the original consonantal structure of the original Egyptian, while persons of the same name are distinguished by roman numerals or letters according to a basic system that has been developing within Egyptology since the 1970s (see Dodson and Hilton 2004: 39).

Dates are given in Egyptian terms, comprising the king's regnal year together with the month and day. The Egyptian year was divided into three seasons, in succession *ȝḥt*, *prt*, and *šmw*, each of which were divided into thirty days; the year ended with five feast days. A correlation with years BC that represents the current broad consensus is provided in Appendix 2, but it should be noted that the absolute chronology of the period prior to 690 BC remains a matter for debate, and that the dates quoted could potentially be moved downwards by a number of decades.[1]

Square brackets in names and translations normally enclose parts of the text that are damaged or missing in the original, and are accordingly shown as either restored (e.g. Amen[meses]) or unrestorable (e.g. Amen[. . .]).

When giving bibliography for monuments and texts, references are generally restricted to Porter and Moss, various dates, and Kitchen 1968–90, which provide all substantive references down to their dates of publication; additional references provided are generally to works published subsequently. Translations and commentaries to texts published by Kitchen are being made available in his companion volumes, Kitchen 1993ff(a) and (b).

MAPS

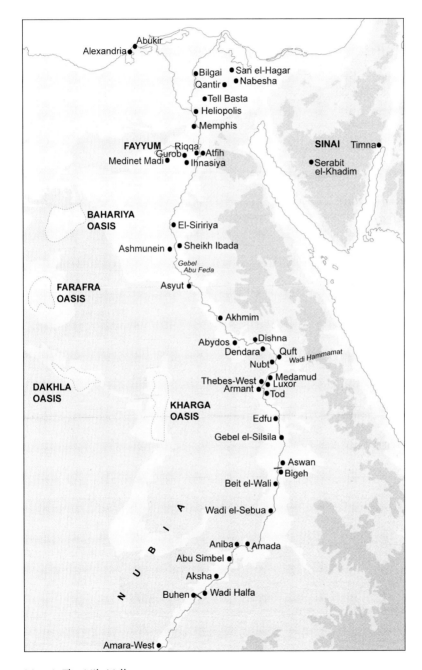

Map 1. The Nile Valley

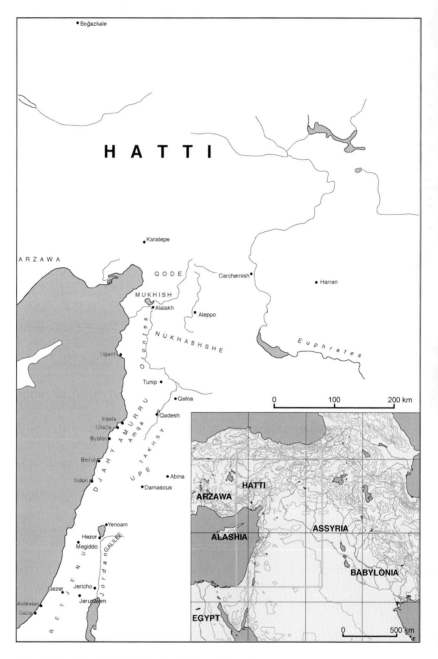

Map 2. The Near East during the thirteenth century BC

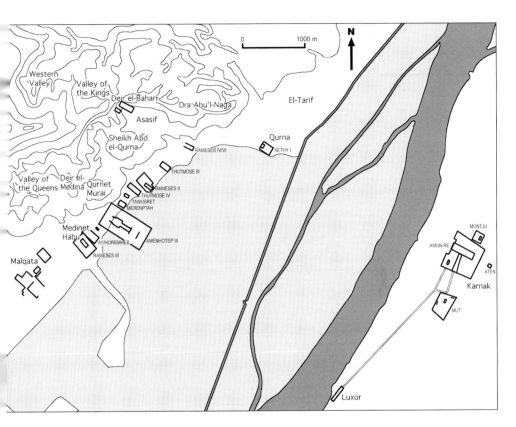

N

0   1000 m

Western
Valley
Valley of
the Kings
Deir el-Bahari
Dra-Abu'l-Naga
El-Tarif
Asasif
Sheikh Abd
el-Qurna
Qurna
SETHY I
RAMESES IV/VI
THUTMOSE III
Valley of
the Queens
Deir el-
Medina
Qurnet
Murai
RAMESES II
THUTMOSE IV
TAWOSRET
MERENPTAH
Medinet
Habu
AY/HOREMHEB
AMENHOTEP III
RAMESES III
Malqata
MONTJU
AMUN-RE
ATEN
Karnak
MUT
Luxor

Map 3. Thebes

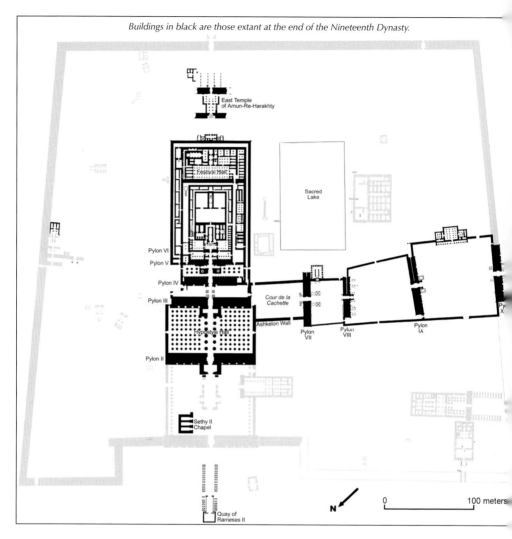

Buildings in black are those extant at the end of the Nineteenth Dynasty.

East Temple
of Amun-Re-Harakhty

Festival Hall

Sacred
Lake

Pylon VI
Pylon V
Pylon IV
Pylon III

Cour de la
Cachette

Pylon
X

Ashkelon Wall

Hypostyle Hall

Pylon II

Pylon
VII

Pylon
VIII

Pylon
IX

Sethy II
Chapel

N

0   100 meters

Quay of
Rameses II

Map 4. The temple enclosure of Amun-Re at Karnak

INTRODUCTION:
THE GLORY YEARS

A t some point during his reign of probably three decades,[1] Horemheb appointed as vizier one Paramessu, of whom two scribal statues were found just inside the gateway of Pylon X at Karnak.[2] From these we learn that he was the son of a Troop Commander (*ḥry-pḏt*) Sethy (A),[3] and that as well as being vizier he was Deputy of His Person in Upper and Lower Egypt (*idnw n ḥm.f m šmꜥw tꜣ-mḥw*), Overseer of the Priests of All the Gods (*imy-r ḥmw n nṯrw nbw*), and Noble in the Entire Land (*iry pꜥt m tꜣ r-ḏr.f*). These titles closely mirror those held by Horemheb during Tutankhamun's reign and, given that Paramessu was to succeed Horemheb as king Rameses I, it is clear that his titles are to be understood as marking him out as the heir to the throne. Thus, in the absence of any living children, it would seem that Horemheb had turned to an old military colleague to follow him as king—especially as Paramessu had a son, the future Sethy I, and possibly already a grandson, the future Rameses II.[4] In doing so, Horemheb continued the military tradition that had dominated Egypt since the demise of the female king Neferneferuaten, probably the former queen Nefertiti, in Tutankhamun's third regnal year.[5] Unfortunately, there is no evidence as to how early in Horemheb's reign Paramessu's nomination occurred. It is possible that Paramessu was joined as (northern?) vizier by his son Sethy, on the basis of the evidence of a rather curious retrospective document dating to Rameses II's reign.[6]

1

On (or possibly shortly before[7]) Horemheb's death, Paramessu, under the name of Rameses (I), became king. However, his reign was short: his monuments are rare, with only one dated example (from Year 2),[8] while his tomb arrangements were improvised.[9] The idea that at some point he shared the throne with his son Sethy I has been a moot point, but it seems most likely that during the life of his father Sethy acted merely as his deputy, rather than as a formal coregent.[10]

Once actually king, Sethy I had a reign that now seems to have lasted just over a decade, rather than the somewhat longer periods that used to be proposed by scholars.[11] It saw, however, large-scale building works throughout Egypt,[12] restorations of Amarna Period mutilations,[13] and campaigns into the Levant. These were at least in part the latest episodes in Egypt's currently volatile relationship with the Hittites of eastern Anatolia, a relationship which had been badly upset by the events surrounding the death of Tutankhamun. Then, a Hittite prince had been sent to Egypt at the request of Tutankhamun's widow[14] to take the throne of Egypt, but had died en route. Convinced that his son had been killed by the Egyptians, Shuppiliumash I had then launched hostilities against Egyptian possessions in northern Syria.[15]

Unfortunately, little is known of events during the following few decades, although some kind of treaty may have been established between Egypt and Hatti—and then broken—under Horemheb and his Hittite contemporary, Mursilish II (c. 1303–1283).[16] However, with Sethy I's accession, reliefs at Karnak provide new data, including actions in Year 1 to quell disturbances in Palestine, followed by expeditions into Syria to confront the Hittites, especially in the area of Qadesh (map 2; fig. 1).

In his Abydos temple, Sethy I provides us with the first surviving depictions of a royal prince whose image was placed on a temple wall by virtue of his princely status. There, he is accompanied in front of the famous so-called "King List" by his son Rameses (A): indeed, it is the prince who actually reads the prayer to which the great list of ancestors is appended (fig. 2).[17] It is quite possible that this is very much intentional, signifying the union of the new parvenu dynasty with the glorious past, not only in the person of the current king, but the king-to-be as well.

That this king-to-be might have been crowned and given a kingly titulary as a "prince regent" during Sethy's reign was for long something approaching orthodoxy. However, it now seems much more likely that Rameses II assumed a kingly dignity only after his father's death,

Fig. 1. Part of the battle reliefs of Sethy I on the exterior of the north wall of the Hypostyle Hall at Karnak. The small figure behind the king's chariot was originally that of a senior army officer named Mehy, but was ultimately changed into one of crown prince Rameses.

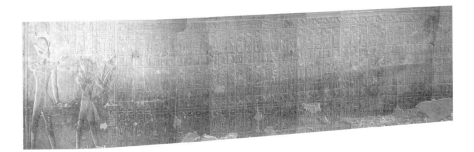

Fig. 2. The king list in the temple of Sethy I at Abydos, with crown prince Rameses reading the prayer of which the king list forms part.

but at the same time stressing his link with Sethy in the continued construction of the various monuments left unfinished on the elder king's death.[18]

Sethy I appears to have died after eleven years on the throne.[19] That this was unexpected is suggested by the large amount of unfinished work that seems to have been inherited by his son, although the latter may well exaggerate the unfinished and neglected state of Sethy's monuments in a text he inscribed in his father's temple at Abydos.[20]

The earliest monuments of the new king, Rameses II, are marked out by a version of his prenomen, Usermaatre, which lacked the epithet "-setepenre" that would become standard in all mentions of the king after III šmw 26 of Year 2.[21] One of the earliest of Rameses' commissions was the rock-cut temple of Beit el-Wali. The decoration of the forecourt shows scenes of a campaign in Nubia in which the king's eldest sons are given important roles (figs. 3–4).[22] This takes the princely depictions under Sethy I a step further, as they are now shown sharing the minatory role of the king himself by virtue of their princely status. Thus, the eldest son, Amenhirwenemef,[23] and the fourth son, Khaemwaset (C),[24] are shown in their chariots in the battle scene, while Amenhirwenemef is also depicted, presenting tribute to his father. No such roles are attributed to royal sons in previous reigns, Rameses' own

Fig. 3. Battle scene at Beit el-Wali, in which Princes Amenhirwenemef and Khaemwaset C accompany their father against the Nubians (cast in Hay Collection, Department of Ancient Egypt and Sudan, BM).

Fig. 4. Prince Amenhirwenemef presents the viceroy of Nubia Amenemopet and the booty of the campaign to Rameses II (cast in Hay Collection, Department of Ancient Egypt and Sudan, BM).

presence in his father's battle reliefs at Karnak being a secondary insertion (fig. 1).[25] Similar representations are found in various later war-related scenes on Rameses II's monuments, with Prehirwenemef (A) and at least one brother at the battle of Qadesh and Khaemwaset, Montjuhirkopeshef (A), Meryamun (A), Amenemwia, Sethy (B), Setepenre (B) and two others at the siege of Dapur, somewhere in northern Syria.[26]

Even more striking than these depictions, which could be regarded as an extension of the "functional" illustrations of royal sons during the Eighteenth Dynasty (that is, where they appear by virtue of their office—such as high priest—rather than their birth) are the great processions of royal children, which are such a feature of many of Rameses' temples (fig. 5).[27] These were generally placed in the outer courtyard or hall of the temple, apparently arranged in order of birth, and numbering some forty-eight to fifty sons and forty to fifty-three daughters; the numerical uncertainties derive from the damaged condition of a number of the sources. No direct parallels are to be found in any previous Egyptian art, perhaps the nearest being the set of unnamed royal daughters taking part in the jubilee celebrations of Amenhotep III, as shown in the tomb-chapel of Kheruef (TT192),[28] or even the depiction of the sons of Sahure

Fig. 5. a. The sons of Rameses II as shown in the procession of princes in the hypostyle hall of the Ramesseum. b. Detail of Merenptah and his elder and younger brother, with his kingly prenomen added alongside his princely titles and name (now cut out).

in his mortuary temple back in the remote Fifth Dynasty.[29] The repeated depiction of the daughters of Akhenaten may possibly also be a form of prototype, particularly in view of the clear Amarna Period promotion of the royal family as the focus of religious devotion.[30]

This promotion of the concept of a broad "royal family" is perhaps a key to an understanding of the dynastic dynamics of the Ramesside and later periods. Until the Amarna Period, the king stood apart from all others. Usually he was depicted alone or set apart by his superhuman size. Even the queen was usually relegated to subsidiary stature. It was only during the Eighteenth Dynasty that the king's wives and mothers consistently acquired the right to visual near-equality with the pharaoh, a trend that achieved its apogee with the exceptional status accorded to Tiye and Nefertiti.

Prior to the reign of Rameses II, the idea of a "royal family" is perhaps made most concrete in a series of three-dimensional representations. On a colossus from Medinet Habu, Amenhotep III sits beside an equal-size queen Tiye, while around their legs are gathered five of their daughters.[31] Under Rameses II, however, a far more impressive manifestation of the concept is to be seen at Abu Simbel, whose temples are in many ways monuments to the broader royal family—or at least that centered on the king and the more prominent of his first two Great Wives, Nefertiry (D) (fig. 6).[32] At the Great Temple there,[33] figures of Nefertiry, the king's mother, Tuya, and the children of the king and Nefertiry, accompany the four colossal figures of Rameses. All of these subsidiary figures are on a much smaller scale than the colossi of the king, but at the neighboring Small Temple,[34] queen Nefertiry has equality of scale with her husband; the offspring who stand with them on the facade of the temple, though much smaller than their parents, are still of impressive size. In two dimensions, an analogous group of Rameses II, the second Great Wife, Isetneferet (A),[35] and their children together, is to be found at Gebel el-Silsila.[36]

Such groupings are also interesting in the way they bring out a further new feature of Rameses II's reign. Apparently from the very beginning of his tenure, there were (at least) two Great Wives, initially Isetneferet and Nefertiry, later succeeded by various of their daughters, together with the Hittite Maathorneferure. A sister[37] of Rameses, Henutmire, also became a spouse (fig. 8) and ultimately also made a Great Wife, but exactly when is unclear. Previously one finds little evidence for more than one *simultaneous* chief wife,[38] with the exception of the assumption of the Great Wife title by Amenhotep III's daughters

Fig. 6. The rock-cut temples at Abu Simbel, in many ways the rock-hewn apotheosis of Rameses II, Nefertiry D, and their children.

Sitamun and Iset (C) late in their father's reign.[39] This had not only the effect of expanding the core of the royal corporation, but also had potential implications for the royal succession.

While the mechanism of pharaonic inheritance remains the subject of debate, it seems tolerably clear that the eldest son by the Great Wife was regarded as the heir, albeit subject to some form of public nomination.[40] While that may have provided ultimate certainty, the existence of more than one Great Wife would seem to have held the potential for dispute as to which "Eldest Son" should be nominated as crown prince. That the arrangement seems to have been successful under Rameses II is shown by the way in which the maternity of Rameses II's four successive heirs moved from Nefertiry (Amenhirkopeshef A[41]) to Isetneferet (Rameses B,[42] Khaemwaset C,[43] and Merenptah A) apparently strictly on the basis of birth order; however, the potential for problems is manifest.

Fig. 7. Figure of Maathorneferure, the Hittite wife of Rameses II, as shown on the remains of one of his statues, probably originally erected at Per-Rameses (Qantir), but now at Tanis (San el-Hagar).

Further innovative representations are the images of family members that begin to be found on royal statues. These can be either in three dimensions adjacent to the king's leg (fig. 7),[44] or at the sides of thrones,[45] or of the back pillars.[46] Although typically found on images of the king, a statue of the queen mother Tuya shows her daughter, and the sister-wife of Rameses II, Henutmire (fig. 8).[47]

While represented in those cases by virtue of their

blood, the various royal sons were granted a range of military and sacerdotal posts, including a perpetuation of the Eighteenth Dynasty practice of appointing royal princes to the Memphite and Heliopolitan pontificates.[48] As high priest at Memphis, Khaemwaset became particularly prominent, long before his ultimate—but short—tenure as crown prince.

The key point about all this is that by the end of the reign of Rameses II there was a concept of royalty that extended beyond the conventional divine couple of the king and queen. There now existed a large group of individuals who were very publicly "royal" and belonged to more than one lineage, two of which had nominally the same seniority. The size of, and offices held by, this group must have represented an important parallel administration to the time-honored network of officials. Another more explicit short-circuiting of the usual chains of command is to be seen in the uses made by Rameses II of Royal Butlers (*wbȝw nsw*) in carrying out specific commissions for the king.[49]

Thus, by the end of the reign of Rameses II, there seems to have

Fig. 8. Statue (re)inscribed for Tuya, wife of Sethy I and mother of Rameses II, but probably originally of Tiye, wife of Amenhotep III. The rear pillar has an image of her apparent daughter, Henutmire. The lower part of the figure was restored in the seventeenth/ eighteenth century, Henutmire being given a male kilt in error; from Rome, Gardens of Sallust (Vatican 22678).

been a fundamental shift in the way the royal family fitted into the Egyptian state. No longer was it simply the king who sat at the top of society, below whom operated the various departments of state, but additionally there was also an extended royal family and household that was essentially separate from, yet highly influential upon, what one might call the regular administration. In particular, the royal offspring had become more than just the pool from which the next king was drawn, but a group with a significance of its own, doubtless bolstered by the fact that many of its members held military positions, and a few of them high sacerdotal posts, as well. It is against this background that the upheavals of the latter part of the Nineteenth Dynasty and later should probably be seen.

The first decade of the reign of Rameses II was dominated by his campaigns in Syria, which served in particular, like those undertaken by his father, as vehicles for combating the expansion of Hittite hegemony into areas hitherto regarded as within Egypt's sphere of influence. Most prominent of them was the Qadesh campaign of Year 5 which, although strategically a stalemate, was widely publicized by Rameses as a great victory (figs. 9–10).[50] However, renewed military activity toward the end of the next decade was followed by a fundamental change of approach. By Year 20 it is clear that both Rameses and his Hittite opposite number, Hattushilish III, were weary of conflict and willing to recognize the reality of each other's position. Thus a treaty was agreed between the two powers, the Hittite text, engraved on a silver tablet, being delivered to Egypt on I *prt* 21 of Year 21.

Fig. 9. Pylon of the temple of Luxor, added by Rameses II, together with a forecourt, to a monument originally built by Amenhotep III. The pylon was used to display an extensive depiction of the king's battle at Qadesh against the Hittite king Murshilish II.

Fig. 10. Section of the tableau of the battle of Qadesh on the eastern tower of the pylon of the Luxor temple, showing the king charging past the city toward the Hittite army.

Monumental Egyptian versions were inscribed in the temples of the Ramesseum and Karnak (fig. 11).[51]

Rameses II was also militarily active in Nubia and to the west in Libya, but much of his reign was taken up with a massive building program that left hardly any part of Egypt unmarked. Significantly, the political center of gravity shifted to the northeast Delta: here, a vast new residence-city of Per-Rameses was established at what is now Qantir. This lay close to what had once been Avaris (Tell el-Daba), the capital of the Palestinian Hyksos kings of the Second Intermediate Period.[52]

In Year 30, the king celebrated his first jubilee (ḥb-sd); there would be at least a further twelve before the end of the reign. As the king aged it is likely that more and more of his routine functions were carried out on his behalf by the current crown prince, the last of whom, Merenptah, took up the role in Year 55. As such, Merenptah added to his previous titles of King's Son (s3-nsw), Royal Scribe (sš-nsw), and Great Overseer of Soldiers ("generalissmo"—iry-r mšꜥ wr), these other titles: Noble (iry-pꜥt), Chief of the Two Lands (ḥry-tp t3wy), Eldest King's Son (s3-nsw smsw), Heir (iwꜥ), Begotten of Geb (sti Gb), and God's Father Beloved of the God (it-nṯr mrw-nṯr).[53] Monuments from this phase of his princely career comprise a representation before Apis 19.8[54] in the Serapeum

bull-catacombs founded by his brother Khaemwaset,[55] a fragment of statue base[56] and a label-text within the Karnak edition of the Rameses II Qadesh tableaux.[57] It is possible that a statue of an Eldest King's Son Ramessu-Merenptah also preserves a unique writing of his name.[58] Merenptah's role as crown prince was to continue for some twelve years until, during II 𝑧ḥt 3–13 in his sixty-seventh regnal year,[59] Rameses II died. Now in late middle age at best, Merenptah became king.

Fig. 11. The Egyptian-Hittite treaty, as inscribed on the outer face of the western ('Ashkelon') wall of the Cour de la Cachette at Karnak (see also fig. 16).

1 THE REIGN OF MERENPTAH

At one level, the accession of Merenptah was marked by the addition of a uraeus to the brow of a number of his princely representations,[1] and of a new column of text with his kingly titles to the monumental processions of the royal sons in the Ramesseum (fig. 5).[2] At another, it provided the world with its first new king of Egypt for nearly seven decades—a world that was changing fundamentally from that which had existed at the accession of Merenptah's father.

Merenptah adopted the wholly new prenomen Baenre ($b3 n R^c$, "Soul of Re"), plus the alternate epithets "beloved of Amun" (mry-Imn—
[hieroglyphs] or [hieroglyphs]) and "beloved of the gods" (mry-$ntrw$—[hieroglyphs]). For a nomen, he added to his birth name the epithet "satisfied with Truth" (htp-hr-$M3^ct$— [hieroglyphs], and minor orthographic variants).[3] The remainder of Merenptah's titulary showed wide variation between monuments and locations, demonstrating the transition seen during the New Kingdom from the Horus, Nebti, and Golden Falcon names being true and generally immutable "names," to their becoming little more than epithets.[4]

The King's Great Wife was a certain Isetneferet (C). An early assumption was that she was none other than Merenptah's full blood sister, Isetneferet (B), but nowhere does the queen bear the expected resulting titles "King's Daughter" or "King's Sister." Accordingly, it has been suggested that Merenptah might have espoused the like-named daughter of Khaemwaset C, that is, the king's niece.[5] However, this cannot be proved and it is quite possible that she was of non-royal birth,

Fig. 12. Merenptah, Isetneferet, and Sethy-Merenptah A offer to Ptah on a stela inscribed at Gebel el-Silsila by the vizier Panehsy.

married to Merenptah long before he had any thought of succeeding to the throne. Isetneferet C is shown on a pair of stelae in the Eighteenth Dynasty rock temple of Horemheb at Gebel Silsila (fig. 12),[6] as well as in Merenptah's own shrine there (fig. 23)[7] and on the back pillar of a usurped statue of Amenhotep III at Luxor temple.[8] A companion piece has the king's sister Bintanat in the same location; whether this indicates that Merenptah espoused Bintanat, or simply reflects Bintanat's position as a queen dowager of her father, Rameses II, is uncertain.[9]

Of the offspring of Merenptah and Isetneferet, his ultimate heir, Sethy-Merenptah (A),[10] is well known from a broken statuette,[11] a number of his father's statues,[12] stelae at Gebel el-Silsila,[13] his father's battle reliefs (fig. 13),[14] a notation of the verso of the Papyrus d'Orbiny,[15] and possibly a column-drum.[16] A further son, Khaemwaset (D), is shown in the king's Palestinian war reliefs at Karnak (fig. 14; see below),[17] while a daughter, Isetneferet (D), may be named in another papyrus.[18]

The possibility that Merenptah had a third son is raised by five monuments that clearly belong together. They name a prince Merenptah (B) whose titulary differs but slightly from those borne by Merenptah himself before he acceded to the throne (lacking perhaps most significantly "Eldest King's Son"), and like him with uraei added to their brows.[19] Most

Fig. 13. Crown prince Sethy-Merenptah A on a block from his father's battle reliefs at Karnak. His name and titulary have been largely erased.

Fig. 14. Khaemwaset D as depicted in his father's battle reliefs at Karnak.

crucially, two of these monuments are statues of Senwosret I, usurped (apparently for the first time) by Merenptah as king, at which time the prince's inscriptions seem also to have been added.[20] Since Merenptah is hardly likely to have taken over the statues to make them represent himself as king, and also show himself in his former status as a mere prince on the same monuments, the presence of uraei on the brows of the latter images is distinctly problematic.

One possibility is that they all actually represent crown prince Sethy-Merenptah, with the first element of his name for some reason omitted. The other is that the prince was indeed a son of Merenptah whose uraeus was added as a result of some aspect of the family intrigues that came to the surface at Merenptah's death. We will return to this in the following chapters. A prince Ramessu-Merenptah might also have been a son of Merenptah—unless he was actually Merenptah himself before his accession.

Little is known of the events of the first years of Merenptah's reign, apart from some inspections of temples in Years 2 and 3.[21] However, in Year 5 a coalition of Libyans and the so-called Sea Peoples from the northeast Mediterranean[22] made an incursion into northwest Egypt before being defeated at "Perire," a place of imprecise location, but certainly in the southern part of the western Delta.[23] These events were recorded in the king's Great Karnak Inscription and associated reliefs in the Cour de la Cachette in the temple of Amun-Re at Karnak (fig. 15).[24]

Fig. 15. The Cour de la Cachette at Karnak, showing the eastern wall that bears Merenptah's account of his Libyan campaign.

Further military activity was directed to the east and was commemorated in a set of reliefs on the outer wall of the Cour de la Cachette (figs. 16–17). These were carved over part of an unfinished version of the Qadesh reliefs of Rameses II, which were masked in plaster.

Fig. 16. The Ashkelon Wall at Karnak, bearing the victory reliefs of Merenptah and the Hittite treaty of Rameses II (fig. 11). Merenptah's images were carved over what was originally the right-hand part of an unfinished depiction of Rameses II's Battle of Qadesh, continued from the left-hand section on the adjacent outer face of the south wall of the Hypostyle Hall.

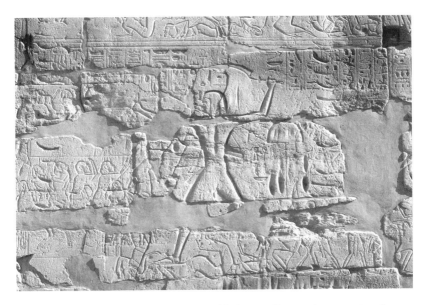

Fig. 17. Detail of Merenptah from the Ashkelon Wall; note the erased and surcharged cartouches.

As Rameses II had himself carved a fresh set of battle reliefs over another part of this palimpsest Qadesh tableau (on the outside wall of the Hypostyle Hall), for many years the Cour de la Cachette-wall reliefs were misattributed to Rameses II as well. However, the latest work on them, by Peter Brand, has confirmed Frank Yurco's earlier assessment that they were certainly carved for Merenptah, whose cartouches were subsequently erased.[25] The campaigning shown in these reliefs seems to illustrate the coda to the victory stelae that were erected in Merenptah's memorial temple (figs. 18–19)[26] and in the southeast corner of the Karnak Cour de la Cachette.[27] In the stelae, the polities of Canaan, Ashkelon, Gezer, Yenoam, and Israel are poetically described as having been defeated by Merenptah, and it appears that at least some of them were depicted in the reliefs.[28] The mention of Israel has long made Merenptah a figure of particular interest to students of the Old Testament, with a large literature that has tried to "prove" various things— in particular that Merenptah might have been the "Pharaoh of the Exodus."[29] In reality, of course, all that the stela indicates is that by Merenptah's time "Israel"—whether just a people or an area—was a recognizable entity somewhere in Palestine.

Fig. 18. The so-called "Israel Stela," containing the victory inscription of Merenptah and including the only ancient Egyptian mention of Israel; from the king's memorial temple at Thebes (Cairo CG34025).

In the same text, Hatti is said to be "at peace": the days of conflict with the Egyptians were long past. Indeed, the Great Karnak Inscription refers to Merenptah sending grain "to keep alive the land of Hatti," which ties in with other data suggesting that at this time the Hittite territories were suffering from famine.[30] In addition to these northern entanglements, a group of stelae of Year 6 at Amada, Amara West, Aksha, and Wadi el-Sebua refer to the suppression of a rebellion in Wawat (northern Nubia) the previous year.[31]

Fig. 19. View of the ruined forecourt of the memorial temple of Merenptah, with a cast of the Israel Stela placed in its original position.

The building works of Merenptah were widespread, although a considerable number of his monuments from the northern Delta were clearly moved and/or usurped by later rulers.[32] Some presumably derived from the former site of Per-Rameses,[33] where Merenptah's presence is indicated by a statue base.[34] Other material comes from the southern Delta, running on into the area of Heliopolis, where various fragments of a temple of the king have been revealed.[35]

Moving now into the Nile valley, at Memphis the king's monuments centered on a large palace with an adjacent temple at Kom el-Qala.[36] Additionally, a number of items are known from the entrance and southern edge of the Fayyum, where the temple at Medinet Madi received attention,[37] and a number of monuments at Ihnasiya (Herakleopolis).[38]

A rock chapel was created at El-Babein, near El-Siririya,[39] while a little further south, Merenptah continued his father's work at Sheikh Ibada (Antinoë),[40] and decorated parts of the pylon and hypostyle hall of the temple of Amun at Ashmunein (Hermopolis), erecting at least one colossus there.[41] At Abydos, the king once again continued the work of his predecessors, in particular decorating parts of the Osirion, left blank since Sethy I's death nearly seven decades earlier,[42] and adding statues and texts to various sanctuaries around the site.[43] An Eleventh

Dynasty chapel at Dendara, erected by Montjuhotep II, was restored,[44] with some work also undertaken at Quft (Koptos), Nubt, and Medamud.[45]

As was the case with his predecessors, Merenptah's largest surviving body of work is to be found at Thebes (map 3). His activities at Karnak (map 4) centered on the decoration of the Cour de la Cachette and adjacent walls to commemorate his military victories (see above, p. 16), together with a statue and a few other additions to standing monuments nearby.[46] There is also material from the Montju enclosure to the north of the Amun temple, and the Mut complex to the south.[47] In the other great sanctuary at Thebes-East, the temple of Luxor, Merenptah usurped statues of both Amenhotep III and Rameses II, as well as adding his names to various parts of the temple.[48]

The king's memorial temple at Thebes-West was built just north of that of Amenhotep III and employed many blocks salvaged from that building, including the stela from which the temple's edition of the Israel Stela was created (fig. 19).[49] Merenptah's temple, whose plan followed the pattern established by Sethy I and Rameses II (fig. 20), was largely destroyed in antiquity; only the foundations and fragments of stone elements surviving, including various statues (fig. 21–22). The construction of the temple was carried out in at least two phases, one presumably beginning at the opening of the reign,

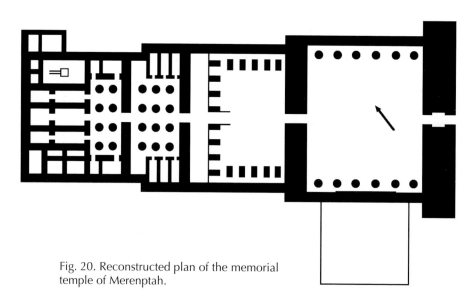

Fig. 20. Reconstructed plan of the memorial temple of Merenptah.

Fig. 21. Fragments of statuary recovered from the memorial temple of Merenptah and reassembled *in situ*.

and one perhaps commencing around the epochal Year 5. The latter phase included the replacement of the First Pylon—originally of brick—with one of stone and an enlargement of certain elements of the temple structure.

South of Thebes, a range of sites preserves traces of Merenptah's activities, including Armant (where he usurped a group of Eleventh Dynasty statues of Montjuhotep III),[50] Tod, Edfu, and Aswan.[51] Most significant is a series of monuments in the quarry

Fig. 22. Upper part of a statue bearing the name of Merenptah; from the second courtyard of his memorial temple (Cairo CG607).

region of Gebel el-Silsila, comprising a number of reliefs and inscriptions within the rock temple of Horemheb, placed there by the vizier Panehsy (fig. 12),[52] and a chapel at the southern extremity of the eastern portion of the site (fig. 23).[53]

The officials of Merenptah's reign were headed, since at least Year 2,[54] by the aforementioned vizier, Panehsy. He is known from a range of material, including the inscriptions at Silsila noted above, a block statue from the Montju enclosure at Karnak,[55] a stela from the temple of Thutmose III at Deir el-Bahari,[56] and a number of pieces of sculpture from Deir el-Medina found in the chapel area north of the village and in the sanctuary of Ptah and Mertseger on the path south to the Valley of the Queens.[57] Panehsy was also the addressee of a letter from the Deir el-Medina Scribe of the Tomb, Qenhirkopeshef,[58] and he is recorded as visiting the king's tomb site in Year 7.[59] By the following year, however, a new vizier, Pensekhmet, had succeeded him in office.[60] A vizier Merysekhmet is known from a Year 3 that could be that of Merenptah, but could instead belong to the period directly

Fig. 23. Shrines of Rameses II (left) and Merenptah (right) at the southern end of the western sandstone quarries at Gebel el-Silsila.

after Merenptah's death.[61] If he dates to Merenptah's reign, Merysekhmet would presumably have been Panehsy's northern counterpart in the split vizierate that had been established during the Eighteenth Dynasty.[62]

At the departmental level of government, in Year 7 the Overseer of the Treasury was one Tjay, who had been succeeded no later than the following year by a certain Merenptah (i).[63] The granaries remained under the administration of Siese (iii), a native of Asyut who had held this responsibility since the time of Rameses II.[64] In the royal household, Merenptah retained the secretary Tjay-To who had served him while a prince,[65] alongside the Royal Table-Scribes Amenemheb and Ahautynefer.[66] A series of five Royal Butlers are known: Rameses-userpehty,[67] Merenptah-emperptah,[68] Pentaweret (in Year 1),[69] Rameses-heru/Penhudjari[70] and—best-attested of all—Rameses-emperre/Meryiunu/Ben-tjana. The last proved to be one of the two great survivors—along with the vizier Hori I—in what was to be a chaotic age: both were still in office under Rameses III.[71] Interestingly, the last two Royal Butlers named were clearly of foreign extraction, as is demonstrated by their names,[72] while the "loyalist" names borne by the first two probably also conceal foreign roots. We will return to the matter of "foreigners" in senior court positions in the next chapter (see p. 72).

Only an Army Scribe, Khaemtjitry, is known from the military hierarchy,[73] while a Royal Envoy Wennefer also attests to foreign affairs management.[74] The Chief of Madjay (police) was a certain Huy, who was also an Overseer of Works.[75] The works portfolio at Memphis and Heliopolis was in the hands of Maya, who had performed the role under Rameses II.[76]

The high priesthood at Memphis also remained unchanged across the reigns, in the person of Hori (A), the king's nephew and son of the great Khaemwaset C.[77] Hori's own like-named son, Hori (I), would later serve as vizier through the reign of Rameses III (see pp. 72, 75, 85, below).[78] However, had Khaemwaset outlived Rameses II, Hori A with his elder brother Ramessu (C)[79] would have been in line for the throne: it is clear from this and other examples that a prematurely deceased crown prince did not pass his rights on to his own sons; rather, the succession devolved on the next-senior son of the living king. Thus, Merenptah had replaced Khaemwaset as crown prince, just as many years earlier Amenhirkopeshef A had been replaced on his death in turn by his brothers Rameses B and Khaemwaset C—not by his own son Sethy (C).

At Karnak, Roma-Roy had also been appointed as high priest back in the reign of Rameses II, probably quite late on.[80] He then served throughout Merenptah's reign into those of his immediate successors.[81] The Third Prophet of Amun Amenhotep also seems to have spanned the reigns,[82] while the Fourth Prophet Raia may also have served Merenptah.[83] Material also survives naming high priests of other cults who are datable to the reign.[84]

In the far south, it is uncertain whether the last Nubian viceroy of Rameses II's reign continued in office under his successor.[85] However, two viceroys are known to have served under Merenptah: Messuy and Khaemtjitry. The former is shown in a number of cases explicitly associated with the king, in particular on the Old Shellal Road at Aswan where he is shown before the chariot-borne pharaoh (fig. 24).[86] He is also attested by kneeling, cartouche-worshiping figures in the temples at Aksha[87] and Amada[88] and a faience plaque from Aniba,[89] plus other items not mentioning a king. These include a kneeling figure carved in the Beit el-Wali speos,[90] a mention on a subordinate's tomb-doorjamb from Aniba,[91] a possible offering stand from Amada,[92] plus shabtis from Wadi el-Sebua[93] and Aniba.[94] The existence of shabtis does not necessarily mean that Messuy died as mere viceroy: such items could be produced many

Fig. 24. Graffito from a granite boulder showing Messuy before Merenptah in his chariot; Aswan, Old Shellal Road.

years in advance of their eventual use, or be used for votive purposes: for example, by various Ramesside dignitaries at the Serapeum.[95]

A graffito on a granite boulder on the island of Bigeh[96] places the damaged name of Messuy[97] directly below another boulder with a cartouche that is possibly readable as that of Sethy II.[98] However, the two sets of hieroglyphs face in opposite directions, and there seems to be no obvious link between the two graffiti, other than their common location; there is thus no evidence that Messuy's term of office extended beyond Merenptah's death.[99]

On the other hand, while most of Khaemtjitry's monuments as viceroy, at Buhen, the great Second Cataract fortress that played an important role in the viceroyalty of Kush (fig. 25), also date to Merenptah's reign,[100] there is also a single piece[101] that seems to place him also in office under Sethy II (fig. 26).[102] He would therefore seem to have replaced Messuy before the end of Merenptah's reign. No direct evidence exists as to when the changeover took place, but one wonders whether it could have been connected with the change in both the vizierate and the Treasury in Year 7/8 (see above, pp. 22–23). Might

Fig. 25. The fortress at Buhen, originally built during the Middle Kingdom, and still a key stronghold of the viceroy of Nubia during the New Kingdom. Many important monuments of the late Nineteenth Dynasty derive from here.

Fig. 26. Stela from Buhen, dedicated by Khaemtjitry, and showing (probably) Sethy II worshiping Horus, Lord of Buhen (exc. no. 1745).

that period have seen a top-level purge by the king? As we shall see, there seems to have been a degree of posthumous hostility toward Merenptah—and the former viceroy Messuy seems to have been among those involved (see next chapter).

Little else is known about events during the years following Merenptah's military activities of Year 5. Indeed, what dated material survives, derives from the activities within the workmen's community at Deir el-Medina—a source which, however, is to become of fundamental importance in disentangling the events that followed Merenptah's demise.[103]

During those years the community was engaged in the construction of Merenptah's tomb, now numbered KV8.[104] It broadly conforms to the revised royal tomb layout established in Rameses II's KV7, but further enhances its symmetry around the axis (fig. 27a).[105] Decoratively KV8 follows what was now the convention, employing the Litany of Re in the outer parts, with the remainder of the decoration centering on the

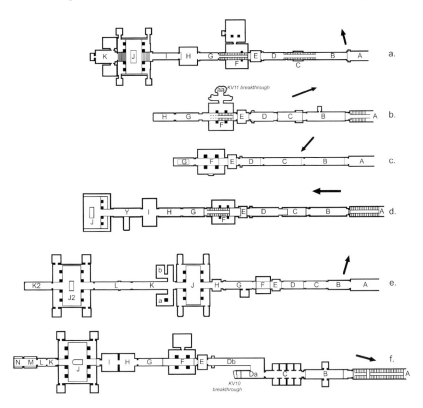

Fig. 27. Plans of the tombs of the kings of the late Nineteenth Dynasty and beginning of the Twentieth in the Valley of the Kings:
a. Merenptah (KV8)
b. Amenmeses (KV10)
c. Sethy II (KV15)
d. Siptah (KV47)
e. Tawosret/Sethnakhte (KV14)
f. Sethnakhte/Rameses III (KV11)

Fig. 28. Left-hand part of the entrance to the tomb of Merenptah (KV8), showing the king being greeted by Re-Harakhty and the beginning of the Litany of Re.

Amduat and Book of Gates (fig. 28). One of the most notable features of the tomb is the number of sarcophagi employed in the royal interment. During the reigns of Sethy I and Rameses II the stone outer sarcophagi had been abandoned in favor of an alabaster outer coffin and, presumably, a set of wooden sarcophagi/shrines. This is reversed with a vengeance in KV8, no fewer than three granite outer cases being employed, along with the alabaster outer coffin.[106]

The innermost sarcophagus had actually been made for Merenptah while he had been crown prince.[107] It is rectangular, and is unusual in having its lower margin adorned with paneling, seemingly imitating certain coffers of the late Twelfth Dynasty.[108] The lid, dating to the period after Merenptah's accession is, however, purely New Kingdom in its form, the first of a new royal design that features a three dimensional Osirian image of the deceased upon the top surface. This sarcophagus was contained within one of the cartouche-plan that had been standard for royal sarcophagi since the time of Thutmose III, with the exception of the late Eighteenth Dynasty.[109] Once again the lid was adorned with a recumbent figure of the king, and the coffer with extracts from the Books of Gates and Amduat. This was in turn enclosed in a gigantic outer rectangular sarcophagus: it seems that a casing of such huge dimensions was not initially planned, since various decorated doorjambs had to be cut away to allow its passage down the tomb and were then repaired. Aside from the remains of these sarcophagi, only a few items have survived from Merenptah's burial. Of his alabaster outer coffin, only a few fragments are known.[110] Likewise, his canopic chest is represented by only a few disparate fragments; some shabtis are extant.[111]

The king's last recorded date seems to have been IV *3ht* 7 in Year 10.[112] His death apparently came just over three months later, as III *prt* 16 saw the announcement of Sethy II's accession.[113] Therefore Merenptah's burial will have followed within the next two months.[114] It is not known how long he remained undisturbed in his tomb, but at some point the body (fig. 29) had to be rewrapped, with the addition of a hieratic docket that named "King Baenre" (his prenomen), and was reinterred in the tomb of Amenhotep II (KV35).[115] In any case, this must have occurred before or during the reign of Pasebkhanut I, as the innermost sarcophagus was extracted from KV8 and transported down to Tanis for use in his tomb there (NRT III).[116] To facilitate its removal the coffers of the outer two sarcophagi were demolished, the floors probably being removed for re-use as stelae.[117]

The mummy's age at death has been estimated from the examination of x-rays as being "45:0–50:0" years;[118] however, as is noted below (pp. 80–81), the validity of these estimates has been questioned, and it is possible that the body is of a considerably older man. Certainly, Merenptah seems to have been born before Year 20 of Rameses II, and thus must have been somewhere between his late fifties and seventy when he died.[119]

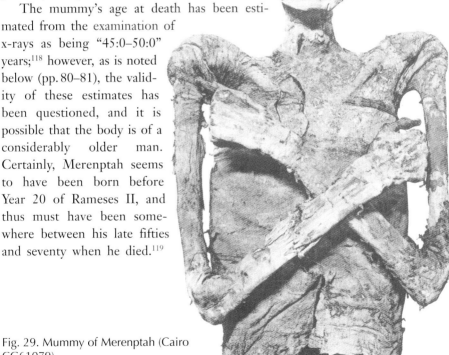

Fig. 29. Mummy of Merenptah (Cairo CG61079).

2 AFTER MERENPTAH

There seems little doubt that crown prince Sethy-Merenptah A was Merenptah's intended successor, as proclaimed visually in his numerous representations on his father's monuments (see pp. 14–15, above); likewise, his equation with king Sethy II seems incontrovertible.[1] As crown prince, he held the full range of titles that went with such a status during the Ramesside Period: Noble, Chief of the Two Lands, King's Scribe, generalissimo, and Eldest King's Son.

However, it is also clear that a considerable number of the surviving monuments of Sethy II (see below, pp. 40–41, 50–55) were usurped from a king Amenmeses whose reign certainly also postdated that of Merenptah. Two basic scenarios have been devised to account for this.[2] The first posits that Amenmeses managed to seize the throne on Merenptah's demise, immediately denying Sethy his dynastic rights: Amenmeses will then have ruled the whole country for some four years until displaced by Sethy II, who then ruled for six years. This was for long the generally adopted solution. The other scenario takes the view that Sethy-Merenptah A did indeed directly succeed his father, but was displaced from (at least) Upper Egypt by Amenmeses in his second regnal year. Sethy would then have ultimately regained power throughout the country, to rule alone for just over a year before his death.

Other scenarios have been produced in the past, when the problem was further complicated by the observation that in KV14 in the Valley of the Kings (the tomb of Tawosret, a wife of Sethy II),

Sethy II's cartouches had been carved over those of a king Siptah (fig. 90). This was taken, not unnaturally, as implying that Siptah had preceded Sethy on the throne. However, with the ultimate recognition that Siptah was actually Sethy's successor (cf. pp. 83–85, below), it was realized that this was a situation analogous to the replacement of Hatshepsut's cartouches by those of Thutmose I and II[3]—that is, a politically unacceptable ruler was suppressed in favor of a more politically acceptable predecessor.[4]

A simple Merenptah–Amenmeses–Sethy II succession has the attraction of apparent neatness, but in practice raises major issues as to the dynamics of the situation, and in particular Sethy II's status during Amenmeses' period of rule: Sethy's hostility toward Amenmeses is made concrete by the violence with which the latter's cartouches have been hacked out on a number of monuments (e.g. figs. 66–67). In favor of the theory of Amenmeses directly following Merenptah is the fact there are no wholly unequivocal examples of monuments of Sethy II being appropriated by Amenmeses or officials transitioning directly from the reign of Merenptah into that of Sethy II.

However, as noted above (pp. 24–26), it seems likely that the Nubian viceroy Khaemtjitry served both Merenptah and Sethy II. In addition, a good case can be made for equating him with the man of the same name who became Amenmeses' vizier (see below, pp. 44, 58–60)—and as such is unlikely to have then regained the viceregal post under Sethy II! As for the reuse of monuments of Sethy II by Amenmeses, there is at least one piece where this may well have occurred—but it can no longer be proved, since the object in question, a statue base belonging to Liverpool City Museum, was lost as a result of the bombing of that institution in 1941, without ever being photographed.[5] Nevertheless, a drawing published in 1839 and verbal and sketched observations by nineteenth- and twentieth-century Egyptologists together clearly show that the piece had ultimately been usurped by Amenmeses. However, the palimpsest traces are problematic, suggesting that the piece was made under Merenptah, recarved under Sethy II, and then usurped again under Amenmeses (see fig. 47, below).

Another monument that is difficult to square with the "simple" succession is the tomb of Sethy II (KV15: fig. 27c).[6] The state of this sepulcher is very strange, with a number of clear discontinuities.[7] First, after the outermost walls of the tomb had been laid out and carved, work came to a stop while the Litany of Re was being carved in the second corridor (C), leaving the remainder of the composition merely sketched out in red ink.

Decoration was later resumed, but further work was done neither on the Litany, nor on carving the other decoration that had been sketched out prior to the interruption of work (reaching into D). Rather, work began by adorning the pillared hall (F) with some low-quality relief-work that contrasts very strongly with the fine style seen in the outer parts of the tomb (fig. 30); this was not, however, ever finished. This second cessation of work seems to have coincided with the king's death and the urgent need to immediately prepare the tomb to receive a burial. Thus, the corridor leading from the pillared hall (G), which should ultimately have given access to the burial hall, was itself converted into a burial chamber through the addition of some crude paintings and the introduction of what would have been the innermost of a nest of sarcophagi (fig. 31).[8] Presumably at the same time, the square room before the pillared hall (E), which would normally have housed the protective "well," was painted with two-dimensional representations of the three-dimensional statuettes of the king and deities that were typically included among the furnishings of New Kingdom royal burials (figs. 32–33).[9] Such representations in two-dimensions are unique to KV15, and one wonders whether their depiction implied an

Fig. 30. Pillared hall of KV15.

Fig. 31. Improvised burial chamber of KV15, containing the broken lid of the king's inner sarcophagus. The coffer is missing and the outer case was probably completed for a later king.

unavailability of actual statuettes at the time of the burial.

To the evidence provided by these successive changes in the approach taken to the decoration of the tomb must be added the fact that in the outer parts of the tomb—essentially those which had been carved according to the original project—the cartouches of the king had been erased and later reinstated (fig. 34). The orthographies of the original and replacement cartouches differ from one another wherever the two versions can be made out, especially in the form of the ⟰ (mn)-sign.

Taken together, it seems clear that the stopping of work on the Litany of Re and the erasure of the cartouches are somehow connected, and that this phenomenon is best explained by the king's overthrow, at least in the Thebaid.[10] Similarly, the restart of work and restoration of names fits well with a restoration, the fresh decorative approach suggesting straitened circumstances and perhaps poor health on the part of the king. KV15 is thus a significant piece of evidence in favor of Sethy II directly succeeding his father, only to be displaced by Amenmeses after a fairly short period on the throne.

A further set of data in support of this sequence of events derives from documents found at Deir el-Medina, among which survive many of the day-to-day documents required for running the tomb-builders' community there.[11] Scrutiny of these records reveals a number of facts of value in assessing the relative chronological positions of Sethy II and Amenmeses.

First, the ostracon on which the report of Sethy II's accession is recorded (see p. 29, above) was used subsequently for noting sickness-absences that included the community's Chief Workman, Neferhotep (ii—in office since the last years of Rameses II)[12]—who was killed during Amenmeses' control of Thebes (see p. 58, below). As the ostracon shows that Neferhotep was alive under Sethy II, the latter's accession must have preceded Amenmeses' seizure of power.[13]

Second, Years 3 and 4 of Sethy II are apparently completely absent from the Deir el-Medina dossier, as are the last months of his Year 2 and the first ones of Year 5. While Amenmeses claimed four regnal years, only Years 3 and 4 are definitely identifiable as his in the Deir el-Medina records on the basis of the personnel mentioned.[14] These various Year 3 and 4 citations all sit neatly within the gap in attestations of Sethy II's date-lines.[15]

Fig. 32. The "well room" of KV15, showing images of the gilded statuettes of the king that would normally have formed part of the royal funerary equipment.

Third, a radical change in personnel at Deir el-Medina is recorded in Years 5 and 6 (of Sethy II).[16] This is again highly supportive of Amenmeses' status as a rival to Sethy II and a return to power by the latter that may have seen a "purge" of those who had adhered to his erstwhile rival.[17]

These data allow one to undertake a back-calculation that seems to place Amenmeses' first claim to kingship about five months after the death of Merenptah.[18] But where did he claim it, and how did his power expand? The presence of a stela of Amenmeses' Year 1 at Buhen (see below, pp. 47–48) clearly indicates that the area around the Second Cataract was an early stronghold, but eight months later, on II ꜣḥt 25 of Sethy II's Year 1, the latter was still recognized at Abu Simbel,[19] only sixty kilometers to

Fig. 33. Gilded statuettes of the kind depicted in KV15 as found in Tutankhamun's KV62, as displayed in the Egyptian Museum, Cairo.

Fig. 34. Upper part of the first—and finest—of the decorative tableaux on the left-hand wall of the first corridor of KV15. Its texts were originally carved in raised relief on a raised background—just visible at the top left. However, those between the king and the god were erased—the scarring caused by the removal of the panel is still visible—and later reinstated in sunk relief.

the north. The presence of a Year 2 stela of Sethy II at Amada[20] is a further indication that the expansion northward was slow at first. As late as IV *prt* of Sethy's Year 2, a stela at Gebel el-Silsila, 120 kilometers south of Thebes, could still be dated by his reign.[21]

As far as the limits of Amenmeses' control are concerned, his most northerly attestation is an inscribed jar found at Riqqa, near the mouth of the Fayyum.[22] Based on this, one might suggest that Amenmeses' ultimate Egyptian realm corresponded roughly with that later controlled by the Third Intermediate Period Theban High Priests,[23] leaving a rump Lower Egyptian regime under Sethy II based in the Delta at the royal residence at Per-Rameses,[24] and embracing the Memphite region, but not much further south. On the other hand, the jar may have been traded from further south, and could thus have no direct bearing on the northern extent of Amenmeses' domain.

But who then was Amenmeses, who was seemingly in a position to displace a king like Sethy II, to all appearances a legitimate heir of apparently impeccable lineage? There have been various suggestions over the decades, principally that Amenmeses might have been descended from one of the elder sons of Rameses II whose heirs had been excluded from the throne by their premature death (cf. pp. 23–24, above), or from one of Rameses' daughters (cf. pp. 41–42, below). Another alternative could be to link Amenmeses with the anomalous uraeus-wearing figures of Merenptah B (see above, p. 37), making Amenmeses a putative son of this prince, with the uraei added by Amenmeses to mark out his father's status.[25] However, there are no parallels for the latter,[26] while the monuments of Merenptah B all lie in the northeast Delta—well outside the known territory of Amenmeses.

Aside from the king himself, the person in the Egyptian state who had the greatest military establishment was the viceroy of Nubia. That Amenmeses might have been one and the same as Merenptah's viceroy of Kush, Messuy (a name which is simply a contraction of a longer name on the DEITY-mose/meses pattern), has been suspected on a number of occasions in the past,[27] although rejected by other scholars for lack of anything other than circumstantial evidence.[28]

However, more solid evidence seems to be provided by the temple at Amada in Nubia (fig. 35), which has a remarkably large number of depictions of Messuy in various parts of the building.[29] Two of them are in surprisingly inconspicuous and inaccessible positions, high up on

Fig. 35. The temple at Amada in Lower Nubia, built during the Eighteenth Dynasty, but particularly rich in late Nineteenth Dynasty inscriptions; the temple is shown here in 1962, before its relocation following the creation of Lake Nasser.

the exterior of the building. One, on the exterior of the hypostyle hall, includes in Messuy's titles the phrase *s3-nsw n ds.f*, "King's Son himself:" this could simply reflect the viceroy's formal title—"King's Son of Kush"—or could it be seen as a hint of royal-princely status on Messuy's part?[30]

The three remaining Amada depictions of the viceroy, however, are in prominent locations. The most important two are at the bottom of the exterior jambs of the main gate, below the original Eighteenth Dynasty adornments: in both cases, the viceroy kneels before a cartouche of Merenptah (fig. 36).

The key point for our current purposes is that directly in front of the foreheads of each of the images of Messuy are a set of cuttings that are difficult to interpret as other than crudely added uraei. Both features are roughly formed, and are susceptible individually to epigraphic "deconstructions" that could make one, if presented with either figure in isolation, extremely cautious about concluding that a uraeus was definitely present.[31] However, taking the figures *together*, it is difficult to believe that *both* doorjambs could have received chance damage such as to make *both* figures look as though they bore uraei. On this basis, it is difficult to avoid the conclusion that uraei were indeed

Fig. 36. Detail of the left-hand doorjamb of the pylon at Amada, showing a figure of Messuy, with an apparent uraeus added to his brow.

added to the brows of the images of Messuy on the outside of the main gateway of the Amada temple.

No such features, however, can be traced on any of the other extant representations of Messuy.[32] In some cases, this could simply be a function of their location: indeed, the two uraei-equipped representations at Amada are, alone of Messuy's viceregal depictions, in prominent positions on the facade of a major temple. They were thus on "public" display, and therefore well-qualified for being singled out for adornment if Messuy indeed became king.

In fact, the parallels provided by representations of other public figures who only later became kings shows that the addition of uraei to early representations was a relatively rare and inconsistently applied phenomenon. Looking at a range of mid/late New Kingdom examples— Ay, Horemheb, Paramessu (Rameses I), Merenptah, Rameses IV, VI, and VIII—we find that in only restricted cases were uraei added to old depictions. Nothing has been done in Ay's Amarna tomb (although since it was in an abandoned cemetery, this may be less significant), nor on the scribal statues of Horemheb and Paramessu: all of the latter would seem to have had major positions in the Ptah and Amun temples.[33] Royal cobras have been extensively added in the Memphite tomb of Horemheb, but of significance may be the fact that the sepulcher was apparently a local center for the king's posthumous cult.[34] Moving on to the Ramesside princes, Merenptah's case has been noted above, p. 13, while the representations of the three ruling sons of Ramesses III produced during the reign of their father also acquired uraei in certain cases.[35] Of these, the Medinet Habu Procession of Princes presents a situation where particular considerations were clearly involved, and should not be directly compared with the other examples.[36] On the basis of the foregoing, the restriction of added uraei to only the two Amada representations of Messuy should not be regarded as a hindrance to their interpretation as providing important evidence toward his equation with Amenmeses.

But what of Amenmeses' family background, whether or not he had previously been Messuy? We have a number of clues, a particularly suggestive one deriving from a statue belonging to a substantial group erected by Amenmeses at Karnak and later usurped by Sethy II (see below, pp. 51–55). One of these pieces[37] has, behind its left leg, a relief of a woman named Takhat (fig. 37). As originally carved under Amenmeses, the label-text read "King's Daughter and King's Mother," but the latter title was subsequently recarved under Sethy II as "King's Wife."[38] The clear impression given is that with the switch of king represented by the statue, the status, but not the identity, of the lady changed. Now, it is possible that Sethy simply married the mother of his erstwhile opponent on the latter's defeat. However, this seems prima facie rather an unlikely reconstruction—why would Sethy wish to do such a thing? Far more likely, surely, is that Takhat had always been Sethy's wife, and that the usurping Amenmeses was actually Sethy II's own son. That Takhat was someone other than a woman married under dubious circumstances in the wake of civil conflict is also indicated by another Karnak statue, which strongly suggests that she was Sethy's wife before Amenmeses's usurpation.[39]

This piece (fig. 38) has Sethy II's inscriptions replacing those of the earlier owner(s), but throughout its history a figure and the titles of a King's Daughter and King's Great Wife Takhat remained unaltered. This would clearly suggest that Takhat stood in the same relationship to the statue's last owner (Sethy II) as she did to its first. Unless there were *two* queen Takhats, or Sethy II married the widow of a

Fig. 37. Statue of Amenmeses in the Hypostyle Hall at Karnak, with a figure of queen Takhat on the side of the back pillar.

predecessor, it would seem not unlikely that Sethy II had originally made the statue and taken it back again at a later date. Thus, another king must have usurped the piece in the interim, and he can only have been Amenmeses. As Takhat's titles were left untouched, these must have had relevance for Amenmeses, with the further implication that Sethy II and Takhat were Amenmeses's parents.[40]

As for Takhat's origins, her title of King's Daughter makes it fairly clear that she must have been a daughter of either Rameses II or Merenptah—with the possibility that she might have been a royal

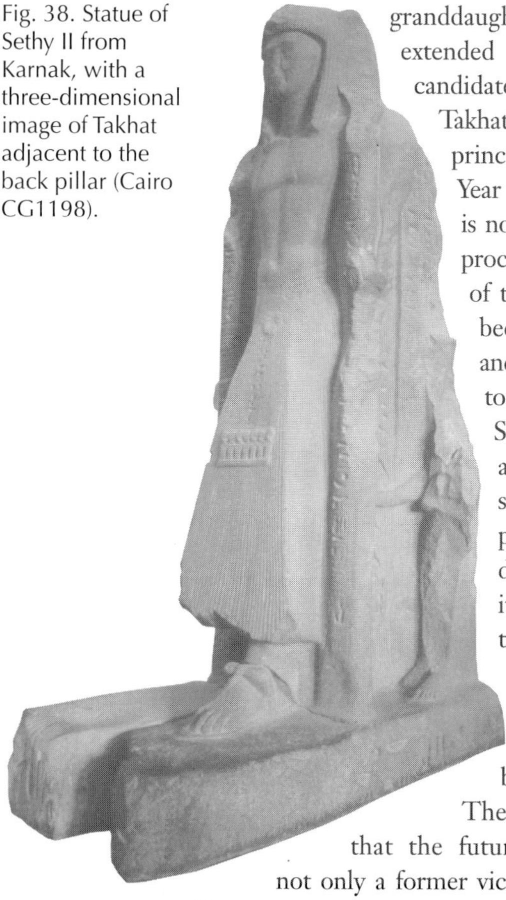

Fig. 38. Statue of Sethy II from Karnak, with a three-dimensional image of Takhat adjacent to the back pillar (Cairo CG1198).

granddaughter, given the occasional extended meaning of the title.[41] A candidate is the King's Daughter Takhat who appears in a list of princesses datable to around Year 53 of Rameses II.[42] As she is not included in the princess-processions of the earlier part of the reign, Takhat will have been a younger daughter, and thus probably quite close to the age of her nephew Sethy II, and thus a suitable match. This conclusion that Amenmeses was a prince of the blood in the direct line makes his ability to launch a claim to the throne far more comprehensible than if he had been merely a scion of what was now a cadet branch.[43]

The foregoing thus suggests that the future king Amenmeses was not only a former viceroy, but also, at the time of his appointment as such, a royal prince as well. Such a combination is apparently unique: occupation of such a senior civil office by a member of the royal family had been unknown since the end of the Fourth Dynasty. Although some members of the royal family had begun to receive posts in the priesthood during the Eighteenth Dynasty,[44] with military appointments added in Ramesside times, there is no evidence for an actual king's son taking such a post as viceroy of Kush. In spite of the inclusion of the element *s3-nsw* (King's Son) in their titles since the time of the very first holder (initially without the modifier *n Kš*), all holders prior to Messuy seem to have been commoners.[45]

On the other hand, if Amenmeses/Messuy had been appointed to the viceroyalty back in the early 50s of Rameses II's reign—before the

death of Khaemwaset C (or possibly even Rameses B)—he
would, although of royal blood,
have been merely a royal great-
grandson, of what was seemingly
destined to be a cadet branch.
It was only the deaths of the
successive crown princes Rameses
and Khaemwaset within a short
span of years that thrust
Merenptah and his descendents
into the kingly limelight.[46] Thus
the appointment of Amenmeses/
Messuy to the viceroyalty would
need not have been a conscious
"royal" appointment—although
the aggrandizement of the
extended royal family, already
noted in the Introduction, may
have played some role in
bringing him into scope for
appointment.

The question of hypothesiz-
ing the motivations behind any
ancient act is always problematic,
and risks straying into historical
fiction. However, a number of
strands of evidence combine to
produce potential hints. The first
is that Amenmeses, as ruler of

Fig. 39. Erased princely figure of
Merenptah on a statue of Rameses II at
Luxor; interestingly, the cartouche
added after Merenptah's accession has
been left intact.

Thebes, showed particular hostility toward Merenptah: at Karnak and
Luxor many of Merenptah's cartouches were very carefully erased and
smoothed, without any trace of recutting as would have been the case
had simple usurpation been the object;[47] there are also examples of his
figure being erased (fig. 39). Interestingly, another person has been the
subject of similar nominal obliteration—Sethy-Merenptah A (the future
Sethy II) in his father's battle reliefs (fig. 13).[48]

Second is the previous observation (pp. 25–26) that Year 7/8 of
Merenptah seems to have seen something of an upheaval in the ranks

of senior officialdom, with the vizier Panehsy and the treasurer Tjay certainly superseded. Might Messuy's replacement by Khaemtjitry have occurred at the same time, making together a series of dismissals that set the scene for events some two years later?

Although Messuy was no longer viceroy at the time of Merenptah's death, he was certainly on good terms with his successor in office, as during Amenmeses' reign his vizier was a certain Khaemtjitry: while it cannot be proven that the viceroy and the vizier were the same man, it seems not unlikely that they were. Thus a credible scenario has Amenmeses' bid for power being based on the forces at the disposal of the viceroy—forces he had once commanded, and who were now commanded by an ally.

If Amenmeses were indeed Sethy II's son, did the latter king have any other offspring—in particular an elder son whose hereditary rights Amenmeses would be in effect usurping? The obvious candidate would seem to be the "Noble, Chief of the Two Lands and Eldest King's Son" Sethy-Merenptah (B) who is depicted standing behind Sethy II in the bark-chapel that the king built in what was then the forecourt of the temple of Amun-Re at Karnak (figs. 40, 71).[49] However, these images are secondary, and to be dated to the very last months of Sethy II's reign (see below, p. 76), making the dating of the prince's career as heir-apparent somewhat problematic. It is thus unclear how Sethy-Merenptah B relates to the story of Amenmeses' rebellion, although it is tempting to suggest that he was one of its early victims.

Apart from the two probable pieces of statuary discussed above (pp. 40, 51–52), and the early phases of tomb KV15, it is difficult to identify monuments of Sethy II that can be assigned confidently to the first part of his reign. Linked with the construction of KV15 are dated materials from Deir el-Medina covering both Years 1 and 2: along with the record of the king's accession (p. 29), there is a note of a visit made by Sethy II to the Theban Necropolis on II *3ḥt* 10 in Year 1,[50] with work underway on the new king's tomb by III *3ḥt* 12.[51] Most interestingly, on I *prt* 8 of Year 2 an order came to "start upon the tomb of the King's Great Wife Tawosret."[52]

This is the first appearance in the record of a lady who would cast a large shadow over the last years of the Nineteenth Dynasty. Although apparently innocuous, the record actually introduces the first known example of a royal wife being granted a substantial, decorated, tomb in the Valley of the Kings. Although its corridors were somewhat lower

Fig. 40. The right-hand wall of the left-hand (Mut) shrine, in the bark-shrine of Sethy II at Karnak (fig. 71), showing Sethy II, followed by a figure of Sethy-Merenptah B, modified from what was originally an image of the chancellor Bay.

and narrower than those of a contemporary king's tomb, the tomb (KV14) seems to have been planned from the outset to have been larger than any previous queenly monument: even such exalted ladies as Amenhotep III's Tiye and Rameses II's own Nefertiry had not been granted such a sepulcher.[53] Tawosret's origins are wholly obscure, the lack of a "King's Daughter" or a "King's Sister" title making it all but certain that she was not of immediate royal ancestry.[54]

One would assume that her marriage to Sethy II was a result of the death of his long-time spouse Takhat. While the fact that Amenmeses would include images of his mother on some of his statues (pp. 40-42) might be used to argue that she was still alive under his regime, the fact that her figures remained intact when the statues were re-used after Sethy II's restoration would suggest that she had played no part in her son's activities—most probably because she was dead. Also, if alive, this would have meant Sethy II having parallel Great Wives—something possessed by Amenhotep III and Rameses II (and later Rameses III, with fatal results), but not a regular pharaonic practice.

On the basis of the foregoing, it thus seems that having succeeded his father Merenptah on his death, only a few months later Sethy II faced a rebellion by his own son, originating in Nubia. Over eighteen months later, Thebes was in the hands of the rebel, whose power seems to have extended ultimately as far north as the Fayyum. The next chapter will consider what we know about Amenmeses' regime.

3 THE REIGN OF AMENMESES

As we have seen in the last chapter, it seems likely that Amenmeses raised his standard of revolt first in Nubia; it is thus appropriate that it is here that his earliest memorial as king survives, in the form of the stela from Buhen (fig. 41). Dated to the second month of a now lost season in Year 1, it showed the king offering to a deity.[1] However, almost all Amenmeses' remaining monuments seem to derive from the period during which he controlled Thebes. From these, the following titulary can be seen (see Appendix 3 for hieroglyphic forms):

Horus	*k3-nḫt mry M3ʿt smn t3wy nb ḥbw sd mi T3tnn*	Strong bull beloved of Maat who makes the Two Lands endure, lord of Sed-festivals like Tjatjenen
Nebti	*wr bi3wt m 'Ipt-swt*	Great of marvels in Karnak
Golden Falcon	*ʿ3 ḫpš sʿ3 W3st n ms.sw*	Great of might who makes Thebes great for he who created him
Prenomen	*mn mi Rʿ stp n Rʿ (mry 'Imn)*	Established like Re, chosen of Re (beloved of Amun)
Nomen	*'Imn(-Rʿ) mss ḥq3 W3st*	Amemn(ra)meses[3] ruler of Thebes

This whole titulary has a distinctly "Theban" flavor, with explicit mentions of both the city itself and Karnak—consistent with Amenmeses being a southern ruler.[2]

47

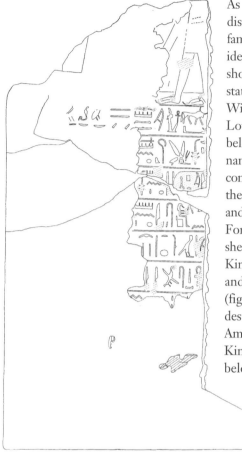

As well as the problems already discussed surrounding Amenmeses' family origins, other issues concern the identity of his spouse. She is actually shown on at least one of the king's statues, with the titles of King's Great Wife and Mistress of Upper and Lower Egypt (fig. 43: see further below, pp. 95–96). Unfortunately, her name has been entirely erased, while a companion piece—presumably showing the same lady—has lost the whole text and most of the female figure (fig. 51). For many years it was assumed that she was probably none other than the King's Wife Baketwernel, whose name and image appear in representations (fig. 44: now almost completely destroyed)[4] in the pillared hall (F) of Amenmeses' tomb in the Valley of the Kings (KV10, fig. 27b: see further below). A depiction of a King's Mother Takhat in the adjacent well room (E: fig. 45)[5] was also assumed to show Amenmeses' like-named mother. However, in 1966 it was pointed out that the decorations of these ladies are painted and carved into a layer of plaster that overlies the decoration of Amenmeses and thus cannot be related to Amenmeses' own decorative scheme for the tomb,[6] confirmed by more recent work in the tomb.[7] In any case, a king's family never has a significant presence (if any) in the decoration of his tomb.[8] It is thus certain that the Baketwernel/Takhat decoration represents a redecoration at some point after Amenmeses' fall.

Fig. 41. Stela with scene of a king offering to deity, dated to Year 1, second month of [...]. The Horus name is that of Amenmeses, although his erased nomen has been replaced by that of Sethy II; from Buhen (exc. no. 1611).

On the other hand, it remains intriguing that Amenmeses' mother was named Takhat, and that one of the "usurpers" of his tomb was a King's

Fig. 42. Aerial view of the temple of Amun-Re at Karnak temple, looking west.

Fig. 43. Remains of a statue of Amenmeses in front of the porch of Pylon II at Karnak. On the right is a drawing of the left-hand side of the back pillar, with an image of his "Great Wife" whose name has, however, been entirely erased.

THE REIGN OF AMENMESES   49

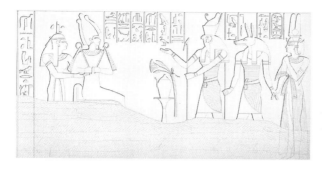

Fig. 44. Image in carved and painted plaster of the King's Wife Baketwernel led by Horus and Anubis toward Osiris and Isis, on the rear wall of the pillared hall of KV10; now largely destroyed.

Fig. 45. Image in carved and painted plaster of the King's Mother Takhat in the "well room" of KV10, now destroyed.

Mother named Takhat. The burial of a lady of this name in the tomb is seemingly guaranteed by the discovery there of a fragment of canopic jar made for a Takhat (title lost), together with remains of a sarcophagus lid that had been reinscribed for a King's Great Wife Takhat.[9] The latter, of a form typical of the Nineteenth Dynasty,[10] had originally been made for a certain Anuketemheb, who had borne the titles "King's Daughter" and "Mistress of the Palace."[11] Anuketemheb's titles have generally been replaced by "King's Wife" and "King's Great Wife," respectively, although "King's Daughter" was left intact in some cases—whether intentionally or not is unclear. All cartouches had been changed. The ongoing clearance of the tomb has also brought to light the remains of the mummy of a woman[12] and debris probably deriving from a coffin.[13]

The absence from the reworked sarcophagus of the title King's Mother, Takhat's title on the wall of the tomb, is curious if the redecorators of the tomb and of the sarcophagus were referring to the same woman. On the other hand the choice of titles used on monuments was not always straightforward.[14] Perhaps the take-over of the sarcophagus was for Takhat (A), wife of Sethy II, following the restoration of her husband, with the tomb of the queen's rebel son allocated to her? Might a subsequent usurpation and redecoration of the tomb during the Twentieth Dynasty[15] have been prompted by the presence within of a (now robbed?) sarcophagus of a lady of the same name (if not same titles) as an intended new occupant? Or could it be that the wall-decoration was applied during what may have been a short-lived "rehabilitation" of Amenmeses soon after Sethy II's death (see pp. 93–94, below)? If Baketwernel's decoration was added at the same time, this lady could have been Amenmeses' wife after all![16]

It must thus be admitted that the affiliations of the Takhat and Baketwernel in KV10 remain problematic.[17] Another potential candidate for Amenmeses' wife may exist in the form of a King's Wife Suterery: she will be discussed below, pp. 90–91.

As already noted, Amenmeses' earliest monument is the Buhen stela; a glass amulet bearing his cartouches also comes from this site.[18] Also in Nubia, Abu Simbel stela 22 shows Amenmeses (his names later replaced by those of Sethy II) slaying foes before Amun (fig. 46),[19] while the king's name was also added to Rameses II's temple at Amara West.[20]

Apart from the vase bearing Amenmeses' name from Riqqa (p. 37, above) and texts added to some standing buildings in the south of Egypt,[21] all his remaining contemporary[22] monuments derive from Thebes. A statue base, apparently usurped from Sethy II, was found at Luxor temple (fig. 47; see pp. 51–52, above), but the most prominent are a series of quartzite statues that were installed in the temple of Amun-Re at Karnak. It is likely that the quarrying of these statues began under Merenptah or Sethy II, and that only the final completion was undertaken by Amenmeses. Ultimately, all these statues were reinscribed for Sethy II, generally in a crude style that contrasts with the fineness of the original work; however, two still preserve readable palimpsest traces of Amenmeses' names. These statues now stand in the

Fig. 46. Stela 22 at Abu Simbel showing Amenmeses slaying foes before Amun; below is a figure of the Deputy of Wawat and Treasurer, Mery.

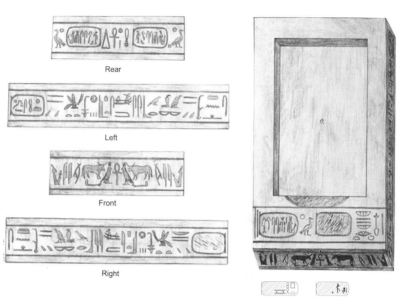

Rear

Left

Front

Right

Palimpsest cartouches on upper surface

Fig. 47. Old drawing, made in the 1830s, of a usurped statue base of Amenmeses from Luxor that was once in Liverpool Museum (M13510) but was lost following bombing in 1941: no photographs of the piece exist. The upper surface had both cartouches recut to give the names of Amenmeses, with the prenomen subsequently erased. The traces of the original names as read prior to the object's loss are shown below the drawing. The original prenomen seems to have been that of Merenptah, the only king of the period with a prenomen beginning with a pair of seated gods, but the visible palimpsest nomen certainly belongs to Sethy II (the full writing of Ptah's name is never found in the nomen of Merenptah himself—cf. p. 13, above). The piece thus seems to have been made under Merenptah, recarved under Sethy II and recarved again under Amenmeses. The texts on the sides of the monument—comprising Amenmeses' Horus and Nebti names, together with both his cartouches—have not been altered: any earlier inscriptions will have been entirely removed beforehand. Only two of Amenmeses' cartouches were ultimately erased after Sethy II's restoration, the rest being left intact for reasons unknown.

Festival Hall (fig. 48)[23] and in the Hypostyle Hall (see above, p. 41 and fig. 37).

Another four statues of this group are also still at Karnak: one in the Hypostyle Hall (figs. 49–50),[24] two in the area of the gateway of Pylon II (figs. 43, 51)[25] and one found north of the Sacred Lake (fig. 52). The last was probably originally the pair of the Festival Hall figure.[26] Three more are now in European collections, two of them colossi (fig. 53–55).[27]

Fig. 48. Kneeling quartzite statue, apparently in its original location in the Festival Hall at Karnak. The names of Amenmeses have been erased and replaced by those of Sethy II. Its close similarity to the statue in fig. 52 suggests that they may have been a pair.

Fig. 49. The second standing figure of Amenmeses in the Hypostyle Hall at Karnak.

Fig. 50. Head of the figure in the previous illustration (MMA 34.2.2).

Fig. 51. Fragmentary statue of Amenmeses in the porch of Pylon II at Karnak, with the remains of a relief of a woman behind its left leg.

Fig. 52. Kneeling statue of Amenmeses found north of the Sacred Lake at Karnak and now in the Hypostyle Hall.

Fig. 53. Seated quartzite statue currently bearing the names of Sethy II but almost certainly made for Amenmeses; from Karnak (BM EA26).

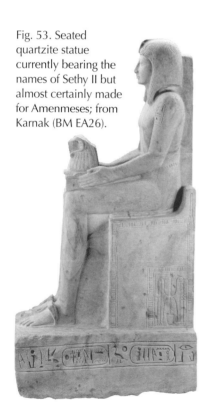

Fig. 54. Colossal quartzite statue usurped by SethyII, almost certainly from Amenmeses; from Karnak, facade of the triple shrine of Sethy II. (Turin C1383).

Likely to be also from Karnak is a fragment of a standing granite (or possibly quartzite) statue of the king, which however is without provenance.[28]

Amenmeses' activity in the area of the Festival Hall is also demonstrated by the addition of his cartouches to a pair of Osirid colossi of Thutmose III at the entrance of the complex (fig.56),[29] with a number of inscriptions added in subsidiary areas (e.g. fig. 57).[30] To the rear of the Festival Hall, in the East Temple of Amun-Re-Harakhty, a bandeau text was added; later usurped by Sethy II, only the initial part of the Horus name of Amenmeses remains readable.[31]

Elsewhere at Karnak, as already noted, Amenmeses undertook a major campaign of erasures of the names of both Merenptah and prince Sethy-Merenptah, although he never seems to have superposed his names over those of the earlier king.[32] Only later were the erased areas filled—by the cartouches of the restored Sethy II. Finally, a doorway directly south of Pylon V received Amenmeses' cartouches.[33]

Amenmeses is also attested at Thebes-West. Although nothing is known of the start of any work on a memorial temple, a tomb (KV10) was begun in the Valley of the Kings and made good progress, extending beyond

Fig. 55. Colossus now bearing the names of Sethy II, made as a pair with the piece shown in the previous illustration and found alongside it (Louvre A24).

Fig. 56. Entrance to the Festival Hall at Karnak, flanked by Osirid colossi of Thutmose III (right-hand figure partly destroyed), usurped by Amenmeses and then Sethy II.

Fig. 57. Amenmeses' reliefs of the Souls of Pe and Nekhen on the north wall in the high-level solar shrine (Room XXXV) in the Festival Hall at Karnak. The cartouches of Amenmeses were ultimately replaced by those of Rameses III, presumably having been erased, but not surcharged, by Sethy II.

the pillared hall before construction was abandoned.[34] Its plan (fig. 27b) followed the basic scheme aspired to by all tombs of the later Nineteenth Dynasty, as did its scheme of decoration (see further pp. 107–9, below).

Otherwise, two stelae were carved into the façade of the main part of the memorial temple of Sethy I at Qurna (figs. 58–59, 87);[35] they were later taken over by Siptah (see pp. 93–94). The right-hand stela calls Amenmeses a "noble youth of Khepri . . . whom Isis nursed in Khemmis to be ruler of all that the sun encircles." This alludes to the youth of the god Horus as a fugitive from his murderous uncle, Seth, in the marshes of the Delta: it has been questioned whether the king is here presenting himself as a legitimate heir excluded from his inheritance.[36]

A fragment of another stela was found near the Ramesseum,[37] while Amenmeses' cartouches

Fig. 58. Location of the right-hand stela (see fig. 87) of the pair inscribed by Amenmeses on the façade of the main part of the memorial temple of Sethy I at Qurna.

replaced those of Merenptah on a pillar base at the Ramesseum itself but were later surcharged by those of a later Rameses (IV?).[38] Dedication-inscriptions were also added to a doorway in the Small Temple at Medinet Habu: here they survive intact.[39]

However, it is the workmen's community at Deir el-Medina that provides the key Theban data for Amenmeses' regime. Apart from the daily documentation that allows the king's period of Theban control to be determined (p. 35, above), other sources dating to the period following Amenmeses' demise are also key. In particular, one papyrus containing a long denunciation of the Deir el-Medina Chief Workman Paneb includes allusions to important events during Amenmeses' control of the Thebaid.[40]

Fig. 59. The poorly preserved left-hand stela at Qurna, showing Amenmeses offering Maat to Amun, Mut, Khonsu, and a king, probably Amenhotep I; it was later usurped by Siptah.

In it, the accuser, the Workman Amennakhte, first states that his brother, the Chief Workman Neferhotep (ii) had been killed by "the enemy."[41] Clearly this was someone sufficiently well-known not to require further definition.[42] Later on, he states that "the Chief Workman Neferhotep complained about [Paneb] to the vizier Amenmose, who punished him. But then [Paneb] made a complaint about the vizier before Mose, and had him dismissed from the office of vizier." Since the vizier was the senior official under the king, this "Mose" can hardly be anyone other than Amenmeses—"Mose" being in any case a well-known diminutive of such names of the form DEITY-mose/meses, of which, as noted above, p. 37, Messuy is simply an expanded variant.[43] Might he also be the individual who caused the slaying of Neferhotep?

The dismissed vizier Amenmose is otherwise known from material in the Deir el-Medina area,[44] a statue base possibly also from here,[45] and a fragmentary libation-bowl.[46] It is unclear whether he might have been Amenmeses' own appointee or had been "inherited" from Sethy II's reign. The context of his dismissal might well suggest the latter.[47]

As his replacement, a man named Khaemtjitry was appointed; as already discussed, he was almost certainly the same man who had succeeded Messuy as viceroy of Nubia, and thus been perhaps the key figure in Amenmeses' bid for the crown. This is certainly supported by the fact that almost all the monuments of the viceroy Khaemtjitry have had his name mutilated, in particular in his inscription on the gateway of the South Temple at Buhen (fig. 60);[48] his other monuments are so damaged that one cannot be certain whether any hostility to the inscriptions' owner was intended.

As vizier, Khaemtjitry features in a shrine that was built somewhere in the Deir el-Medina area (fig. 61);[49] a number of other shrines were also constructed in this part of the necropolis during Amenmeses' time, in particular in the Oratory of Ptah and Mertseger, between the village and the Valley of the Queens (fig. 62). All have been badly damaged by the collapse of overlying strata of rock, Chapel E being reduced to merely the upper part of its stela (fig. 63),[50] with Chapel G preserving only part of its south wall. This includes, however, the remains of a scene of Amun, Ptah, Harsiese, Min-Kamutef, Isis (twice), and Osiris, offered to by a king, who is followed by a vizier and a Deir el-Medina Chief Workman (figs. 64–65). All cartouches have been erased, but were probably those of Amenmeses. While the vizier's name is damaged, the reading '*I[mn-ms]* seems likely. The relief would thus apparently date to the beginning of Amenmeses' regime, before Amenmose's dismissal. The identity of the Chief Workman is uncertain, depending on how the killing of Neferhotep related to the dismissal of the vizier; he could thus be either Neferhotep or his successor Paneb. At least three other fragments are known that probably derive from the one or other of this group of monuments—or another

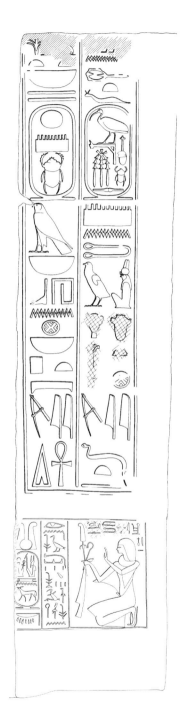

Fig. 60. South doorjamb at the South Temple at Buhen, with an added figure at the bottom representing Khaemtjitry, whose name has been damaged.

Fig. 61. Block from a shrine in the Deir el-Medina area, showing the vizier Khaemtjitry; the prenomen of Amenmeses has been mutilated and later replaced by that of Sethy II. In contrast, the vizier's name was only plastered over, and that of the vizier Parahotep cut on top of it (Chicago OI 10816).

Fig. 62. Oratory of Ptah and Mertseger, between Deir el-Medina and the Valley of the Queens, and containing a number of shrines datable to the late Nineteenth and early Twentieth Dynasties.

Fig. 63. The remains of the stela in Chapel E at the Oratory of Ptah and Mertseger. The lunette shows a king, accompanied by Mut and Hathor, receiving the *ḥb-sd* symbols from Amun-Re and Ptah. The nomen cartouche now reads "Sethy-Merenptah," but the prenomen is Userkhaure-setepenre-meryamun—that of Sethnakhte. All visible names are secondary, and it is likely that the cartouches were originally those of Amenmeses.

Fig. 64. Relief in Chapel G, at the Oratory of Ptah and Mertseger, showing Amun, Ptah, Harsiese, Min-Kamutef, Isis (twice), and Osiris, offered to by a king, who is followed by a vizier and a Deir el-Medina Chief Workman.

Fig. 65. Detail of the Chapel G relief, showing Ptah, Amun, the king, the vizier, and a few traces of the chief workman.

in the same area (figs. 66–68).[51] The king's names appear also in a number of West-Theban graffiti.[52]

Besides the viziers Amenmose and Khaemtjitry, the officials who served Amenmeses are little known. Even the identity of whoever followed Khamtjitry as Nubian viceroy is unknown. We have already met Mery, the Deputy of Wawat on Amenmeses' Abu Simbel stela (p. 62, above). The son of an earlier Deputy and Mayor of Aniba, Harnakhte,[53] Mery left a number of other monuments in Nubia, including his tomb at Aniba (SA7).[54]

In the sacerdotal sphere, Roma-Roy seems to have continued the career that had begun under Rameses II (p. 24, above). Of his inscriptions on the east end of Pylon VIII,[55] those above the doorway have had their cartouches erased (fig. 69). Although it has been assumed that these represent obliterated names of Amenmeses,[56] they are almost certainly those of Merenptah (cf. above, pp. 17–18). However, as undamaged texts and images naming Sethy II were subsequently added above and to the right of the doorway it is clear that Roma-Roy continued in office after Sethy's restoration.

Fig. 66. Limestone block with a scene of Amun, Ahmes-Nefertiry, and Amenhotep I receiving offerings, with a text of Amenmeses: the cartouches have been mutilated and surcharged with names of Sethy II (BMA L68.10.2.[48]).

Fig. 67. Fragment of a stela of Amenmeses, with names hammered out and then overwritten with those of Sethy II (Chiddingstone Castle, Kent, Denys Eyre Bower Collection, as of 2013 on loan Houston Museum of Natural Sciences [04.2013.0460]).

The means by which Amenmeses' regime was brought to an end are obscure. All that one can say for certain is that somewhere between III *ꜣḥt* and I *šmw* in the fourth year since Amenmeses had declared himself king in Nubia, Sethy II was once again recognized in Thebes. Whether this was by means of military action or by political means is wholly unknown. However, there is material that may hint that intrigue could have played at least a part. This will be considered further in the next chapter.

Whatever the means by which he was removed from the scene, the official view of Amenmeses taken by Sethy II's restoration administration

Fig. 68. Fragment of relief showing Amun offering "jubilees" to Amenmeses (formerly Liverpool M13827).

is clearly demonstrated by the mutilation of many of his cartouches (cf. figs. 61, 66, 67). In these cases, they have not merely been erased, but deeply—and roughly—hacked out, making their later surcharge with Sethy II's names difficult. That Amenmeses' names had been singled out for special treatment is shown by one of the Deir el-Medina blocks where, while the king's name has been hacked out, that of his vizier Khaemtjitry has simply been plastered over to allow the block to be recut with the name of his replacement, Paraemheb (fig. 61). The treatment of the vizier's name is a simple case of usurpation; that meted out to the king's cartouche is clearly a matter of *damnatio memoriae*, with ultimate replacement of his names a secondary consideration.

A rather different approach is to be seen in Amenmeses' tomb, KV10. Here there is no vicious hacking of names, but neither is there an attempt to carefully obscure names for easy usurpation. Instead, the vast majority of the raised-relief decoration of the tomb has been sliced off level with the background (fig. 70).[57] This is without obvious parallels, and must have a very particular meaning. It has been suggested that the removal of the decoration in this way was a means of de-activating the "magical machinery" of the tomb, to guarantee that Amenmeses was denied, in death as in life, the royal destiny that he had arrogated though his seizure of power.[58] It has even been speculated that Amenmeses might actually have been buried in this "religionless" tomb;[59] however, that such a rebel could have been allowed to lie in the Valley of the Kings among the legitimate monarchs of Egypt seems most unlikely. Another explanation could be that the walls were being cleared for the tomb's usurpation; however, Ramesside royal tomb decoration is fairly generic, and a usurping king could simply have replaced the names and the relatively small number of depictions of the original owner—just as was actually done with the tomb of Tawosret early in the Twentieth Dynasty (see p. 126), below.

Fig. 69. Eastern end of Pylon VIII at Karnak, showing the figures and texts of the high priest Roma-Roy surrounding the doorway leading to the pylon's interior stairway. The erased cartouches were most probably those of Merenptah. The tableau above, and the text to the right were added under Sethy II (see fig. 75).

As to Amenmeses' personal fate, it is possible that he was killed at the time Sethy II returned to Thebes. Or he may have retreated back into his Nubian heartland and suffered death there some time later. In any case, however, it is unlikely that he survived the end of Sethy II's reign, as a possible later political rehabilitation (see pp. 93–94, below) was not accompanied by a physical restoration as well. Whenever his death occurred, it was probably followed, at best, by consignment to some obscure grave or, at worst, by the body's consumption by fire—the worst possible fate for the corpse of an Egyptian.

In texts written after his demise, where it was necessary to mention his time in power, Amenmeses was explicitly denied any royal status—being simply "Mose" and perhaps also the "enemy" in the denunciation of Paneb (pp. 57–58, above). His oblivion was not complete, however, as the confused listings of the kings of the Nineteenth Dynasty in the surviving epitomes of the third century BC Egyptian historian Manetho[60] include an Am(m)enephthis[61] and an Ammenem(n)es, one of whom (most likely the second) probably conceals a memory of Amenmeses.[62] It is also possible that the story of Amenmeses' revolt contributed to the story of Sethôs and Harmaïs, quoted by the Jewish historian Josephus from Manetho.[63]

Fig. 70. Erased relief of the goddess Maat from the entrance of KV10. The removal of the decoration was done in such a way, however, that most of the motifs and texts are still fully legible.

Indeed, it has been suggested that Amenmeses' memory has survived in a far more universal way, in that his career was transmogrified into the Old Testament story of Jewish history law-giver, Moses.[64] Certainly it is not difficult to see the "Moses" as simply the Egyptian "Mose." However, this connection is beyond proof and such a survival of Amenmeses into world consciousness remains but an intriguing possibility.

4 SETHY II RESTORED

I t is unclear whether the titulary of the restored Sethy II differed substantively from that used in his first years. Only one full titulary is formally dated (to Year 1),[1] and while the king had a number of variant Horus and Nebti names and orthographies of his cartouche names, they cannot at present be shown to be chronologically significant.[2] The range of names used by the king is as follows (see also Appendix 3):

Horus	a.	kꜣ-nḫt wr pḥty	Strong bull mighty in strength
	b.	kꜣ-nḫt mry Rꜥ	Strong bull beloved of Re
	c.	kꜣ-nḫt mk Kmt	Strong bull protector of Egypt
Nebti	a.	nḫt ḫpš dr pḏt 9	Strong of arm subduing the Nine Bows
	b.	sḫm ḫpš dr pḏt 9	Powerful of arm subduing the Nine Bows
	c.	mk Kmt wꜥf ḫꜣswt	Protector of Egypt who subdues foreign lands
Golden Falcon	a.	ꜥꜣ nrw m tꜣw nbw	Great of terror in all lands
	b.	ꜥꜣ nḫtw m tꜣw nbw	Great of strength in all lands
Prenomen		wsr ḫprw Rꜥ stp n Rꜥ/mry Imn	Powerful of forms like Re, chosen of Re/beloved of Amun
Nomen		Sthy mr n Ptḥ	Sethy-Merenptah

69

On III *ꜣḫt* 14 of Year 5 of the restored Sethy II a burial was made in Theban Tomb 26, constructed for the Overseer of the Treasury in the Ramesseum Khnumemheb under Rameses II or Merenptah.[3] The interment was that of the "Superintendent of the House of the Royal Children, who was in the (royal) suite," Qedmerti.[4] Who the "royal children" were is unclear: the only clearly named child of Sethy II is crown prince Sethy-Merenptah B who, as already noted (p. 44), presents a number of problems, which will be discussed just below.

Among the works at Karnak that date to the period following Sethy II's return, one includes a feature that may have a bearing on how the king regained control of the south of Egypt. This is the triple shrine that was erected in front of the Amun temple at Karnak now enclosed in the First Court, added by Shoshenq I (fig. 71). As it stands today, its decoration includes images of the king with his son Sethy-Merenptah B behind him (fig. 40). However, it is clear that the prince's figures and titles have replaced those of another individual,[5] while in some cases the king is followed by a largely blank space where a figure and its texts have been erased (fig. 72).

All figures and texts were originally those of the Great Overseer of Sealers of the Entire Land ("chancellor") Bay. Soon afterwards, they had been

Fig 71. The bark-shrine of Sethy II at Karnak. The rough masonry at the left (west) end is a result of its partial rebuilding in conjunction with the erection of the adjacent Pylon I in the Late Period. The colossi shown in figs. 54-55 were found flanking the entrance to the central shrine.

altered to represent Sethy-Merenptah, the reworked images in the centralchapel being erased at some later date (cf. pp. 93-94). Bay was to play a crucial role in the later history of the Nineteenth Dynasty—and in view of his placement here, seemingly had done so in relation to Sethy II's restoration as well. Such a representation of a noble in direct company of a king in a temple has few parallels—the most obvious one being the God's Father Ay who hovers behind Tutankhamun in a number of Karnak contexts.[6]

Our first glimpse of Bay may come from the earliest part of Sethy II's reign, when a man of that name wrote on an ostracon a short prayer to Amun: "The King's Scribe and Royal Butler of the King,[7] Bay, of Sethy-Merenptah. He says to Amun-Re, King of the Gods: 'Come to me, Amun and save me. I am a visitor from the northern country. Come and let me see the beautiful city, while I see its women.'"[8] This text conjures up—rightly or wrongly—the image of a wide-eyed ingénu on his first trip "up country," interested in both the great

Fig 72. Erased figure of crown prince Sethy-Merenptah B (originally the chancellor Bay) standing behind Sethy II on the left wall of the middle sanctuary of the bark-shrine: the outline of the front of the kilt is very clear.

city of Thebes and its other distractions! Its naïve sentiments seem to sit uneasily with their author's probable role a few short years later.[9]

Bay's parentage may be revealed by a Theban graffito, which was "made by the Royal Butler, Bay, son of Ka[. . .]."[10] Whether the name "Bay" itself may or may not be foreign has been much discussed, as his ethnic origins have an important bearing on the later historiography of the period. In favor of a non-Egyptian origin is Bay's cognomen, Rameses-khaemnetjer: such "loyalist" cognomina are not infrequently found attached to the names of foreigners who entered pharaonic service—in a number of cases as Royal Butlers.[11] If so, we might speculate that Bay, or his parents, had come into Egypt in the wake of Rameses II's campaigns in Syria-Palestine.

As to what lay behind Bay's being granted the signal honor of representation in Sethy II's shrine,[12] a clue may lie in Bay's probable original role as a Royal Butler. As already noted (p. 9), such individuals seem to have been employed as royal representatives in a troubleshooting role by the Ramesside kings, and it was perhaps for brokering some key element of events that led to the downfall of Amenmeses that Bay was granted his representations as the king's closest associate in the Karnak shrine. As such, this role will have been a precursor to his activities during the half-decade that followed Sethy II's death (see next chapter).

Whatever the extraordinary commission held by Bay, the formal governmental structure continued to be headed by the vizier. Not surprisingly, Khaemtjitry was superseded by a new man, Paraemheb (cf. fig.61). The new vizier remained in office until at least Year 6, II šmw 6, when he visited Deir el-Medina for the festival of Amun.[13] Paraemheb features in a number of graffiti left by quarrymen in the Wadi Hammamat.[14] Some name him as vizier, one as both Overseer of Works and vizier, and others simply as Overseer of Works (figs. 73–74); it is unclear whether this indicates that Paraemheb was first Overseer of Works, and was only subsequently promoted to vizier, or whether he always held both posts.

It is possible that Paraemheb left office under a cloud: among accusations leveled against the Deir el-Medina Chief Workman Paneb (cf. pp. 57–58) was that he had given five servants to "Paraemheb, who had been vizier," apparently as a bribe.[15] In any case, Paraemheb was superseded as vizier by Hori I—son of the Memphite high priest Hori A, and thus

Fig 73. Graffito of the vizier Paraemheb in the Wadi Hammamat. The Seth-sign in the king's nomen was erased in Ptolemaic times.

Fig 74. A Hammamat graffito of Paraemheb as Overseer of Works.

great-grandson of Rameses II[16]—before the end of Sethy II's reign.[17] Hori would remain in office until the reign of Rameses III,[18] and one wonders whether his ancestry may have been of help in maintaining his position even after the overthrow of the last Nineteenth Dynasty ruler.

Few other members of Sethy II's revived administration are known. In Nubia, a new viceroy was to be installed in Year 1 of Siptah (see p. 85, below), but nothing is known about who filled the gap back to Khaemtjitry's elevation to the vizierate under Amenmeses. In the palace administration, two personnel of the harem at Gurob (Miwer) are known—its Deputy, Usermaatre-emheb,[19] and its Royal Scribe and Overseer of Staff, Sethy.[20] A Chief Craftsman of the Lord of the Two Lands, Huy, served Sethy II at Per-Rameses, where the lintel of his house doorway was found.[21]

In the priesthood, Roma-Roy at Karnak survived the restoration (cf. p. 62, above) but was soon interred in his monumental tomb on Dra Abu'l-Naga[22] and succeeded by a certain Mahuhy.[23] This succession negated Roma-Roy's expressed desire to pass his office on to "his son,"[24] presumably in the person of the Second Prophet of Amun, Bakenkhonsu (ii), whose figure is mutilated in the scene on Pylon VIII where he is seen accompanying his father (fig. 75); doubtless

Fig 75. The eastern end of Pylon VIII at Karnak, with the tableaux of the high priest Roma-Roy (see also fig. 69), with the mutilated figure of his son, the Second Prophet Bakenkhonsu ii, on the far right.

Bakenkhonsu had been too close to the Amenmeses regime. Up at Memphis, it appears that Khaemwaset C's son, Hori A, was replaced by a new high priest, Pahemnetjer, who may have been a relation, to judge by the existence of a double statue of Pahemnetjer and the vizier Hori I, who was definitely Hori A's son.[25] At Abydos, a high priest of Isis, Wennefer, is known from a number of monuments.[26]

The state of the royal family at the time of Sethy II's return to Thebes is not fully clear, the only secure individual being the King's Great Wife Tawosret who, as already noted (pp. 44-45), had attained her role by Year 2, and whose career would stretch to the end of the dyansty.

Tawosret retained her fine tomb in the Valley of the Kings and is depicted with her husband on a pair of bracelets (fig. 76)[27] that came from a pit-tomb in the Valley of the Kings (KV56). This sepulcher also contained various debris[28] that may have represented the remains of the burial of a child of the couple.[29] On the bracelets, Tawosret has only the title "King's Great Wife:" after Sethy II's death she is found with the additional title of "God's Wife." One would assume that this

Fig 76. Scene from the pair of bracelets found in KV56, showing Tawosret before Sethy II (CM CG52577–8).

had been granted during Sethy II's lifetime,[30] in which case it further marks out Tawosret's exceptional status. While most Great Wives down to the middle of the Eighteenth Dynasty were also God's Wives, this was not generally the case subsequently.[31]

As already noted, the only pieces of evidence for a named child of Sethy II are the secondary representations of Sethy-Merenptah B in the Karnak shrines. As they replaced images of the chancellor Bay (see. pp. 71–72), interpretation is difficult, although there seems no reason to doubt his existence as some have done. It has also been suggested that the changes reflected the prince's birth very late in the reign,[32] but it is also possible that the images memorialised an individual who had died earlier (perhaps an early victim of the Amenmeses conflict?)—but in this case one would wonder what prompted this move, and the concomitant apparent insult to Bay whose power continued beyond the death of Sethy.

Apart from his Karnak shrine, Sethy II erected a pair of obelisks on the Rameses II-built quay at the western limit of the Amun precinct (fig. 77), and nearby a stela.[33] Furthermore, a now fragmentary stela was carved into the west wall of the Cour de la Cachette, comprising a decree apparently aimed against corruption among temple staff at Karnak.[34] Beyond these pieces of work, Sethy II's efforts in the Amun

Fig 77. The quay at Karnak, with the surviving obelisk of Sethy II.

Fig 78. Upper part of a quartzite statue probably usurped by Sethy II from Amenmeses (BM EA26: see also fig. 53).

temple were largely confined to replacing erased cartouches of his father and those of Amenmeses with his own names, adding a few minor additional texts,[35] and usurping the Amenmeses' statuary (see above, pp. 40, 51–55; fig. 78). At Luxor temple, a set of bandeau texts was cut over similar Amenmeses-erased inscriptions of Merenptah around the Rameses II courtyard, the Great Colonnade, and the Sun-Court.[36]

Across the river in Thebes-West, apart from the king's tomb in the Valley of the Kings, only a usurped pillar in the Ramesseum can be identified:[37] no trace of a memorial temple has yet to come to light.[38] There seems no possibility of this putative structure having been built and then usurped by an immediate successor: foundation deposits have been uncovered in the memorial temples of both Siptah and Tawosret which make clear their original ownerships (see below, pp. 106, 114). A series of faience plaques bearing the king's cartouches, certainly deriving from foundation deposits, have been found at Memphis,[39] Karnak,[40] the Ramesseum,[41] and Medinet Habu;[42] the West-Theban may have come originally from Sethy's lost memorial temple. The signs used on the plaques are the same in form as those employed in the later phase of the king's tomb,[43] and thus date to the period following Sethy II's restoration in the south.

North of Thebes, and thus possibly worked on throughout the reign, depending on how far Amenmeses' control actually extended (cf. p. 37, above), is the doorway of the pylon of the temple of Ashmunein (fig. 79).[44] Various minor items also come from north of Thebes,

Fig 79. The remains of the Ramesside pylon of the Thoth temple at Ashmunein, with a large relief of Sethy II on the interior of the gateway.

including the Sinai,[45] the northeast Delta,[46] the apex of the Delta,[47] Heliopolis and Memphis,[48] Atfih, Gurob, and El-Babein,[49] and Gebel Abu Feda, Dishna, and Medamud,[50] mainly in the form of texts added to earlier monuments or minor inscribed items.

Taken together, the paucity of these monuments attests to the limited period of time and resources available to Sethy II; indeed, the king's health may already have been poor when he returned to power in Thebes. In his tomb, the fact that the carving of previously outlined decoration was only recommenced some distance beyond the point where the sculptors had laid down their chisels in Year 2 (cf. pp. 32–33, above) may suggest that a degree of urgency was felt to be appropriate even in Year 5. This impression is reinforced by the fact that this carving was soon terminated, and work switched to the Pillared Hall. The poor workmanship in this room (fig. 30), contrasting with the magnificent relief work in the first corridor (fig. 34), also suggests that attempts were being made to push work ahead as rapidly as possible.

Yet the tomb was still far from complete on I prt 19 of Year 6, when a Deir el-Medina ostracon[51] records that "the Chief Policeman Nakhtmin came, saying: 'The falcon has flown to heaven, namely Sethy; another has arisen in his place.'" Assuming that the king died in the north, it must have taken some time for the news to reach Thebes, and from other evidence it seems that he actually died some time prior to Day 11, possibly on Day 2.[52]

It was doubtless from the moment of this announcement that the hurried preparation was begun of the unfinished passage beyond the pillared hall to take Sethy's burial (fig. 31). The decoration of this space did not follow any previously established scheme,[53] while the presumably simultaneous adornment of the well room (fig. 32) was also unique (see pp. 33–34, above). Apart from his smashed sarcophagus lid, no certain remains of Sethy II's funerary equipment have ever come to light: two fragmentary faience shabtis that have sometimes been attributed to him may actually belong to Sethy I.[54]

The funeral took place approximately three months after the king's death, as recorded in a graffito above the entrance of Tawosret's adjacent tomb, KV14: "Year 1, III prt 11: day of the burial of User-kheper[u]re."[55] It has been suggested that this indicates that the interment took place in KV14 itself, rather than KV15,[56] but given that work continued in KV14 for another eight years (see below, pp. 113–114), it seems distinctly unlikely that the mummy of Sethy II could have been permitted to lie in a place where it would be passed daily by those quarrying the inner part of the tomb. Surely, a more likely explanation is that the notation merely records the funeral of Sethy II in the directly adjacent KV15—the entrance of the as yet unfinished KV14 *would* have been an obvious resting place for those engaged in burying the late king.

Sethy's rest may have been disturbed soon after the placement of his mummy in the tomb, as the Chief Workman Paneb was accused by Amennakhte (cf. pp. 57–58, above) of having not only entered the burial place of Sethy II, and stolen wine and oil, but also apparently of having sat on the king's (occupied) sarcophagus![57] The exact date of this event is uncertain, and may even have been before the final sealing of the tomb.[58]

A visit to the site of the tomb was made by the Butler Sethhirwenemef in a Year 6,[59] probably of Rameses IV,[60] and at some point later the king's mummy was apparently removed from the tomb for its own protection. Certainly a replacement coffin lid was produced,[61] which ultimately ended up placed on the trough of the coffin of Rameses III[62] in a side room of Amenhotep II's tomb (KV35), together enclosing a mummy labeled as that of Amenhotep III.[63] A mummy anciently labeled simply "Sethy" was found in a lidless coffin trough in the same chamber.[64] As Sethy I's mummy was unequivocally found in the TT320 cache, this would presumably identify it as that of the second king Sethy.

When the mummy was unwrapped in 1905 (fig. 80),[65] shirts bearing the name of Merenptah were found among the linen used to rewrap the plundered body, but it was noted that the corpse bore little resemblance to the bodies of the other Nineteenth Dynasty kings. As the head also resembled far more closely those of Amenhotep II and Thutmose IV, it has been questioned whether the mummy might have been mislabeled in antiquity.[66] The body has also been assessed as being that of someone only twenty-five years of age,[67] far too young to fit in with the historical reconstruction offered in the present work.[68]

On the other hand, there are major problems with many of the assessed ages at death for many pharaohs,[69] and in this connection it is instructive to consider the implications of the studies carried out on over a thousand sets of eighteenth- to nineteenth-century AD human remains recovered from the crypts of Christ Church, Spitalfields in London.[70] Of these, nearly half were of individuals whose age at death was indicated by coffin plates. These studies involved determining the apparent

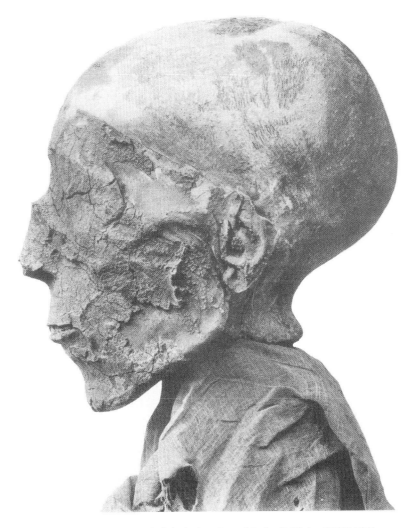

Fig 80. The mummy anciently labeled as that of Sethy II (Cairo CG61081).

ages of the remains on the basis of the usual anatomical metrics. However, when these ages were compared with the explicit ages recorded on the coffin plates, it was seen that "there was a systematic error which depended on the age of the individual, those under forty being over-aged, those over seventy being under-aged . . . . Less than 30% of the sample were correctly aged—i.e. to within five years of the real age; but 50% were assessed to within ten years, and three-quarters to within fifteen years of the correct age . . . ."[71] Among cases of under-aging, individuals who were known certainly to have died in their late eighties, or their nineties, appeared according to the anatomical criteria to be in their sixties, or in one case late fifties!

However, while this resolves some of the age problems with the royal mummies,[72] stretching the assessed twenty-five years of "Sethy II" to the later middle age likely to have been reached or exceeded by the real Sethy II seems difficult: the 1905 visual examination assessed the body as "young or middle-aged."[73] The identification of the mummy must thus remain doubtful.[74]

5 SIPTAH

The report of the death of Sethy II on I *prt* 19 of the king's Year 6 is repeated a few lines later in the same ostracon, but with the year now written as "1": there could be no break in the pharaonic succession.[1] The name of the successor seems to have been unknown to Nakhtmin when he made his report to the Deir el-Medina crew, but three months later, IV *prt* 21 saw the commissioning of the tomb of "Sekhaenresetepenre, son of Re, lord of appearances, Rameses-Siptah."[2]

This same king is represented or named in a number of other places: on rock-cut stelae (dated to his Year 1) at the northern and southern extremities of the terrace of the Great Temple at Abu Simbel (fig. 81),[3] on a pillar base at the Ramesseum,[4] on a pilaster at Buhen (fig. 99a)[5] and on two jars from the Serapeum.[6] But who was he and how did he come to succeed Sethy II? Indeed, the discovery of the aforementioned ostracon in the early twentieth century had been something of a surprise, since one of the Serapeum vessels had been found inside a jar of the time of Rameses IX:[7] on the basis of this, historians down to 1912 had assumed that Rameses-Siptah had been Rameses IX's successor and had thus entered the history text books as "Rameses X" (the kings nowadays numbered "X" and "XI" being then "XI" and "XII").

A further complication arises when we find Rameses-Siptah soon vanishing from the record—the first regnal year mentioned in the Deir el-Medina and Abu Simbel sources being the highest known. Instead, monuments appear bearing the name of one Akhenre-setepenre

Fig. 81. Detail of a rock-cut stela on the north terrace of the Great Temple at Abu Simbel, showing Rameses-Siptah offering to Amun.

Merenptah-Siptah. Were they the same person, or different individuals? A number of pharaohs are known to have changed one of their cartouche names—for example, Pepy I and Rameses IV took new prenomina; Amenhotep IV became Akhenaten—but there are no other examples of a king swapping *both*. However, "both" Siptahs shared a Horus name, *k3 nḫt mry Ḥꜥpi*, as well as a vizier (Hori I) and a viceroy of Kush (Sethy Q). There are also no overlaps of surviving year-dates (Rameses-Siptah is only known in a Year 1; Merenptah-Siptah's known years begin with 3). Thus, the general view is now that one king radically changed his cartouche names a year or so into his reign.

Another surprise occasioned by the ostracon was that (Rameses/Merenptah-)Siptah had been the successor of Sethy II. On the basis of a number of cases where (Merenptah-)Siptah's cartouches have been overwritten by those of Sethy II (see below, p. 111), scholars concluded that (Merenptah-)Siptah must have been a *predecessor* of Sethy. As a result, some scholars experimented with schemes that involved separate kings Rameses-Siptah and Merenptah-Siptah.[8] However, the cumulative evidence of the ostracon and the points mentioned in the previous paragraph have long since produced a consensus that there was indeed but one king Siptah,[9] leaving another explanation to be sought for the amended cartouches.

The two titularies of Siptah run as follows (see Appendix 3 for hieroglyphic forms):

Horus	*k3-nḫt mry Ḥꜥpi s'nḫ t3 nb m k3.f r' nb*	Strong bull beloved of Hapi who causes the whole land to live by means of his *ka* every day
Prenomen	*sḫꜥ n Rꜥ mry 'Imn/stp n Rꜥ*	He who is made to appear by Re, beloved of Amun/chosen of Re
Nomen	*Rꜥ mss s3 Ptḥ*	Rameses-Siptah

Horus *a*	*k3-nḫt mry Ḥꜥpi s'nḫ t3 nb m k3.f r' nb*	Strong bull beloved of Hapi who causes the whole land to live by means of his *ka* every day
b	*k3-nḫt mr T3ṯnn*	Strong bull beloved of Tjatjenen
c	*k3-nḫt wr pḥti mi 'Imn*	Strong bull great of strength like Amun
d?[10]	*ḫꜥ m 3ḫ-bit*	Appearing in Khemmis

Nebti	$s\ʒ\ 'Iwnw$	Made great in Heliopolis
Golden Falcon	$[...]\ mi\ it.f\ R^c$	[. . .] like his father Re
Prenomen	$\ʒ\underline{h}\ n\ R\ stp\ n\ R^c$	Effective spirit of Re, chosen of Re
Nomen	$mr\ n\ Pt\underline{h}\ s\ʒ\ Pt\underline{h}$	Merenptah-Siptah

As to the way in which Siptah was raised to the throne, a trio of inscriptions provides much food for thought. One is a relief on the Old Shellal Road at Aswan showing the king with the Nubian viceroy, Sethy, before him in an attitude of praise (fig. 82).[11] Behind Siptah is the "chancellor, Sole Companion, who casts out falsehood and promotes truth, and who established the king in the seat of his father, Great Chief Treasurer of the Whole Land, Rameses-Khaemnetjer Bay." In the rock temple at Gebel el-Silsila, Bay once more appears behind the king, calling himself again one "who established the king on the seat of his father, whom he loved" (fig. 83).[12] Bay's boast is particularly striking: for a man to claim to have been installed in his father's place by a king is quite normal; for a man to have installed a *king* in *his* father's place is without parallel: king-making was theoretically a job for gods. Indeed, some researchers have attempted to turn the passage around and make Bay merely the recipient of the usual favor.[13] However, the Egyptian clearly and consistently

Fig. 82. Graffito on the Old Shellal Road at Aswan, showing the viceroy Sethy before Siptah and the chancellor Bay.

Fig. 83. Detail of a stela in the rock temple at Gebel el-Silsila, showing Siptah accompanied by Bay.

reads *smn.ti nsw r st it.f*, which is difficult to twist from its *prima facie* meaning.[14] Furthermore, if the alternate translation were correct, one would have expected the scenes to have been in some way concerned with Bay's appointment—which they are not. The most straightforward reading of Bay's boast is that he is indeed presenting himself as nothing less than a "king maker." Could his presence alongside Sethy II in the Karnak shrine (pp.71–72) indicate that he had previously been that king's (re)maker? And what might his erasure there say about that relationship?

In the light of this, Bay's further claim at Aswan to be responsible for "driving out falsehood and emplacing truth" is potentially telling, as is the way his figure, as large as that of the king, hovers behind Siptah in a relief at Deir el-Bahari (fig. 84).[15] Here, Bay states to the king: "I placed my eye upon you when you were alone ... I protected all your people ...."

That Siptah required the services of such an individual to "place him on the seat of his father" has clear implications for his background. As we have seen, the royal succession was usually based on the previous king's nomination, and/or the new king's carrying out of his "father's"

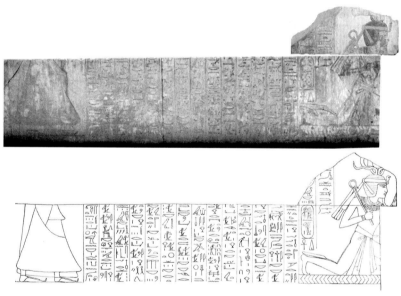

Fig. 84. Relief on the rear of the podium in the Eleventh Dynasty mortuary temple of Montjuhotep II at Deir el-Bahari, with Siptah (his cartouche partly mutilated) followed by Bay. The text comprises Bay's praises of the king (head of king NMS A.1907.712.6).

funeral. There seems no obvious role for an inter-
mediary, such as Bay claims to have been, if Siptah
had simply been a son of Sethy II, as has often been
implicitly assumed.

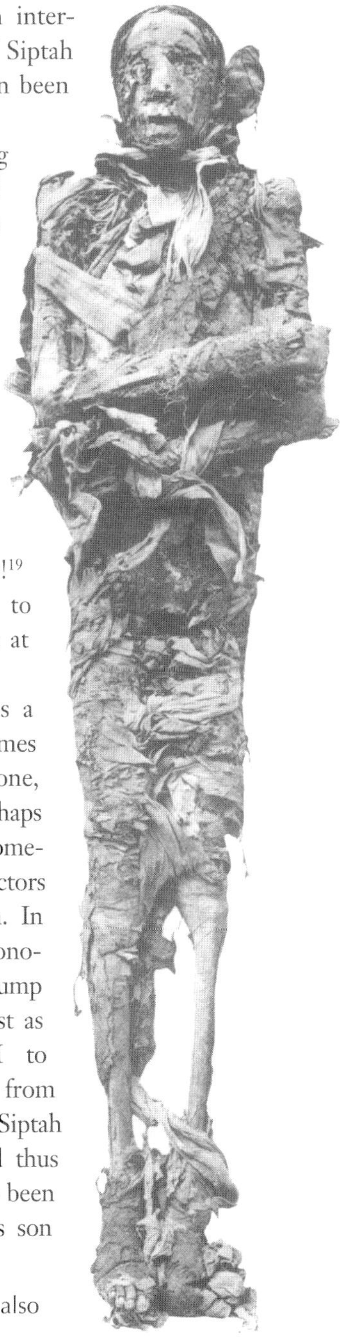

On the other hand, Siptah was clearly young
at his accession. A mummy anciently labeled
with the prenomen of Siptah[16] was found in the
tomb of Amenhotep II (fig. 85).[17] X-ray studies
published in 1980 estimated his age as "20:0–
25:0" years old,[18] which would place his accession in his mid or even late teens. However,
as noted above (pp. 80–82) there remain major
issues as to the validity of many of the ages of
death calculated on the basis of modern skele-
tal metrics, including one teenager who had
been assessed on the basis of anatomical metrics as apparently in her mid thirties![19]
On this basis, one would be strongly tempted to
reduce Siptah's age at death into his later teens at
the very least.

In either case, at his succession Siptah was a
child or not much more. Given the difficult times
that had preceded his assumption of the throne,
might Siptah have been Sethy II's heir but—perhaps
faced with a resurgent Amenmeses?—required someone to guarantee his accession? Yet there are factors
that argue against Siptah being Sethy II's son. In
particular, during the Twentieth Dynasty, chronological presentations of past kings pointedly jump
from Sethy II to Sethnakhte (see fig. 125),[20] just as
earlier listings jump from Amenhotep III to
Horemheb, omitting the intervening kings from
Akhenaten to Ay.[21] This certainly suggests that Siptah
was in some way regarded as illegitimate, and thus
unlikely to have been Sethy II's son. It has also been
wondered whether he could have been Sethy's son

Fig. 85. The mummy of Siptah (CM CG61080); see also
fig. 98.

but in some way disqualified by virtue of an unacceptable mother. In particular, it has been speculated that Siptah's mother might have been Syrian, invoking a passage in the Great Harris Papyrus that provides a glimpse of the Twentieth Dynasty's view of the period directly preceding the seizure of power by Sethnakhte (see further pp. 120–121, below):

> Then another time came consisting of empty years when Irsu, a Syrian (*irsw w^c ḫꜣrw*) was among them as a chieftain, having made the whole land into subjection before him; each joined with his companion in plundering their goods, and they treated the gods as they did men, and no offerings were made in the temples.[22]

While most scholars are in agreement over the basic thrust of the passage,[23] there have been various views regarding "Irsu." Is "Irsu" a real name or a circumlocution meaning something like "he who made himself"—making the whole string imply "the upstart Syrian"?[24] The second perhaps fits better with Egyptian views on the importance of a name, and their preference for using such circumlocutions for those whose memory was reviled—for example "the Enemy from Akhet-Aten" for Akhenaten[25] and "He who is hated by Re" for one of the alleged conspirators against Rameses III.[26]

A number of researchers have proposed that Siptah was this "Syrian,"[27] and a recent alternative translation of the "empty years" passage emends parts of the text so as to read:[28]

> Another time came into existence after that time with empty years, since "That one who reigned for six years"—a Syrian—was among them as a ruler.[29]

Siptah's last known regnal year is 6,[30] while his putative Syrian blood would come from first identifying the king with a prince Rameses-Siptah, known from a number of monuments,[31] and then interpreting the name of that prince's mother, Suterery, as being a Syrian one.[32] But does this interpretation of the passage really ring true where a child-king is concerned? Such individuals are usually either the legitimate heir or sufficiently close to the succession to be manipulated onto the throne under a broadly credible pretext. This is unlikely to have been the case with someone who could be so easily characterized as a mere "Syrian"—and in any case would having a Syrian mother nullify being the son of a king of Egypt? Rameses II had no problem with making his Hittite bride[33] a King's Great Wife, with all that might imply for the rights of any children he might have with her.

In addition, although Siptah was ignored by the Twentieth Dynasty kings (see above, fig. 125), there is no sign of posthumous venom that such a depiction in the Great Harris Papyrus would surely imply; indeed, as will be discussed on p. 122, some of his cartouches were seemingly restored under Sethnakhte. It would thus seem unlikely that Siptah was the subject of the Twentieth Dynasty's retrospective.[34]

A far more likely candidate would seem to be the chancellor Bay, who may well have been of Syrian extraction (cf. p. 110, above). As we have already seen, he had the power to make kings and, as is discussed below, is shown as virtual coequal of a queen dowager and had a tomb of royal dimensions in the heart of the Valley of the Kings. Especially given his ultimate violent fall from grace (see p. 107, below), it would be odd if such a man *did not* find a place in the demonology of later regimes, and "Irsu" seems to fit the bill perfectly.

Returning to the identity of Siptah's mother, the equation of king Siptah with prince Rameses-Siptah is by no means certain: the latter could quite well be the like-named twenty-sixth son of Rameses II.[35] If Suterery were thus to be ruled out, however, other candidates for the mother of king Siptah are distinctly limited in number. A King's Wife and King's Mother Tiaa is named on a number of fragmentary objects from Siptah's tomb (KV47), including pieces of an alabaster canopic chest and a piece of wood, and thus might at first sight seem a prime candidate.[36] However, it now seems that all these items found i n KV47 may have been washed in by the ancient floods that wrecked the lower part of the king's sepulcher, via an accidental breakthrough into the adjoining Eighteenth Dynasty tomb KV32 (fig. 94).[37] This burial place was that of Tiaa, mother of Thutmose IV,[38] and thus the KV47 material has no bearing on the identity of Siptah's mother. Tawosret has also been put forward as a can-didate,[39] but nowhere is she called "King's Mother" in her numerous monuments of Siptah's reign, which makes it certain he was not her son.

What then of Siptah's father? Sethy II could still remain a candidate, in spite of the curious matter of Bay's involvement in Siptah's enthronement. However, in the State Museum of Egyptian Art in Munich there is a sadly mutilated statue that may provide the key (fig.86).[40] A tiny, headless

Fig. 86. Mutilated statue, originally showing Siptah on the lap of an adult—possibly Amenmeses (Munich Gl.122).

figure of a king seems to sit on a strange complex of podia, identified as Siptah by his prenomen-cartouche

Closer inspection also showed that the strange podia were actually the remains of a much larger seated figure, upon whose lap the small image of Siptah had been perched. All evidence of the identity of the large figure had been removed, leading to a debate as to who s/he might have been: mooted options included Tawosret,[41] Sethy II,[42] and Bay.[43] Cyril Aldred, however, noted[44] that the figure could only be a male, with the royal throne making a pharaoh a certainty—ruling out Bay. Moreover, the figure was a king, and one whose memory was later execrated—which ruled out Sethy II, and left Amenmeses apparently the only credible candidate. As Siptah is shown perched on his knee, the implication was clear: Amenmeses was Siptah's father.

If this were indeed the case, a number of pieces of the jigsaw would fall neatly into place, explaining both Siptah's need for Bay's aid and making the latter's boast of "placing the king on the seat of his father" concrete. It would also give potential significance to a variant Horus name that may have been briefly adopted by Siptah, $ḥ^c$ m $ꜣḫbit$ ("Appearing in Khemmis").[45] This could allude to the myth of Horus as a young fugitive hiding from his usurper-uncle Seth in the marshes of Khemmis, and link with a similar allusion by Amenmeses himself in his Qurna texts (above, p. 57). These allusions were apparently felt to be applicable to Siptah when the stelae were taken over for him, in what appears to be the only case of Siptah taking over a monument of Amenmeses (fig. 87). On the other hand, the surviving copy of the royal prenomen that accompanies the one attestation of this Horus name appears to be corrupt,[46] and it is possible that the name has nothing to do with Siptah.

What circumstances could have led to Amenmeses' son being placed on the throne so soon after Sethy II's southern restoration? It could be that, although facilitated by Bay (and probably others), the succession was the inevitable result of Siptah's being the only living descendant of Sethy II: who knows what deaths within the royal family may have resulted from Amenmeses' rebellion? Also, might that rebellion not have been aimed at Sethy II as much as at the shadowy crown prince Sethy-Merenptah B? In this context, the erasure of some of the prince's images in the Karnak triple shrine (pp. 70-71) may be suggestive. After all, unless Amenmeses was relying on his descent from one of the younger daughters of Rameses II, or specific divine

Fig. 87. Detail of the right-hand stela in the Qurna temple of Sethy I (see fig. 58), showing Siptah (formerly Amenmeses) receiving a sword from Amun, who is accompanied by Ahmes-Nefertiry, Sethy I, and Rameses II.

nomination, his claim to the throne would have to be based on being the son of Sethy II, even if he were to allege that his brother was somehow illegitimate. This would explain the half-hearted erasures in KV15, and also the lack of any attack on Sethy II's memory by the Siptah regime.

It would presumably have been at this point that the Munich statue was made, to mark this implicit rehabilitation of Amenmeses. Such a posthumous reassessment of Amenmeses' memory may also be reflected in a stela from Abydos (fig. 88).[47] It shows in its upper register priests carrying a divine bark, in front of which is inscribed *'Imn-Rˁ-mss m wiꜣ*—apparently "Amenmeses[48]-in-the-bark," a deified form of the king. If so, it would certainly date to this putative "rehabilitation" period. On the other hand, the royal name may actually be simply a corrupt writing of that of Rameses II.[49]

As Siptah was little more than a child, a regency on his behalf was essential. While commoners could fulfill this role—an excellent example being Horemheb under Tutankhamun—someone of royal status would normally be the preferred choice. Generally speaking, the king's mother was apparently the preferred regent: back in the First and Sixth Dynasties, Meryetneith and Ankhesenpepy II had ruled for their young

Fig. 88. Stela from the Kom el-Sultan at Abydos showing a divine bark that may commemorate Amenmeses—or may simply incorporate a corruptly written cartouche of Rameses II.

sons, Den and Pepy II, respectively. A stepmother could also suffice, the best-known example being Hatshepsut, who was simply regent for Thutmose III for seven years before becoming his fully-fledged core-gent.[50] In Siptah's case, the regency devolved upon Sethy II's widow, Tawosret, since Siptah's own mother—perhaps the wife of Amenmeses depicted on some of that king's statues (figs. 43, 51)—was presumably dead or excluded on political or personal grounds.

Tawosret appears acting as regent on a stela from Bilgai, near Mendes;[51] this records her construction of a monument for "her father," the god "Amun of Usermaatre-setepenre." Although dated to a now lost year of Siptah, Tawosret is the key actor. While her name was erased throughout the stela (as were the names of Siptah), enough survives to show that her principal title used here was almost certainly "The Great Noblewoman of Every Land" (*t3 iryt-p't n t3 nb*). This title and her additional explicit description as the daughter of "Amun of Usermaatre-setepenre," give her a status above that of the vast majority of royal women and inevitably recalls Hatshepsut in the years leading up to her assumption of kingly titles.[52]

As previously noted, Tawosret had had a tomb begun for her alongside that of her husband Sethy II in the Valley of the Kings (KV14: fig. 27e).[53] The carving of the first phase of its decoration, however,

dates to the regency, with both the queen (fig. 89) and her young ward (fig. 90) shown on the walls of the outer corridor (B) offering to various gods.[54] Here, Tawosret bears (*inter alia*) the title "King's Great Wife," and for many years this led to the assumption that Tawosret and Siptah were a married couple, particularly when it was assumed that Siptah had preceded Sethy II on the throne. However, the recognition of the true relative succession of the kings, and of Siptah's youth, indicated that Tawosret's use of the title was far more likely to be because, in her role

Fig. 89. Image of Tawosret from the right-hand wall of the first corridor of KV14, carved during the earlier part of her regency.

Fig. 90. Siptah and the goddess Isis in the first corridor of the tomb of Tawosret (KV14); the king's cartouches were later surcharged with those of Sethy II, although much of the plaster has now fallen away.

as regent, she simply kept the title she had held during her husband Sethy's lifetime. This precisely parallels the situation of Hatshepsut *vis-à-vis* Thutmose III during his earliest years.

However, Tawosret was clearly not alone in her authority, given the unprecedented standing of Bay under Sethy II, his role in Siptah's accession, and continuing status into the young king's reign. The close association between Bay and Tawosret is made apparent in two sets of reliefs added to Nubian monuments by the Troop Commander of Kush, Piay. The first is in the Great Temple at Abu Simbel, where Bay and Tawosret are shown together adoring the name of Siptah (fig. 91);[55] the other comprises the jambs of a doorway in the temple of Amada, previously the favorite place of Messuy. On the right-hand jamb we find an image of Tawosret (fig. 92) and on the other a corresponding figure of Bay (fig. 93).[56] In both sets of reliefs Tawosret and Bay are both shown on the same scale, which according to normal Egyptian practice implies an exceptional parallelism of status between the queen dowager and the chancellor, and thus provides additional support to the equation of Bay with the all-powerful "Irsu."

Fig. 91. Relief added to the inner left jamb of the main door in the Great Temple at Abu Simbel, showing the names of Siptah being adored by Tawosret and Bay.

Fig. 92. Right-hand jamb of the door leading to the rear part of the Amada temple showing Tawosret, shaking a sistrum and with the titles God's Wife, King's Great Wife, and Mistress of the Two Lands.

The parallelism between the two is further emphasized in the Valley of the Kings. Tawosret's tomb had been begun next to that of her husband, Sethy II, in the western extremity of the wadi, where Thutmose I had been laid to rest (in KV38)[57] some two centuries earlier (fig. 94). However, to this marital pair was added a third tomb: that of Bay (KV13: fig. 95–96).[58]

It is unclear whether the construction of Bay's tomb began under Sethy II—in parallel with Bay's commemoration in the bark-shrine at Karnak—or was granted under Siptah; in any case, work on the tomb was under way

Fig. 93. Opposite doorjamb showing the chancellor Bay worshiping the cartouches of Siptah. The Abu Simbel and Amada images were all inscribed by the Troop Commander of Kush, Pay.

during the season of ꜣḫt in Siptah's Year 3.[59] Which ever king was the donor, the honor thus bestowed was wholly exceptional, for although many notables had been buried in the Valley over the decades, the sheer size of KV13 was unprecedented there for anyone other than a king.[60] While burial complexes exceeding its sixty-meter length exist in some Nineteenth Dynasty noble tombs elsewhere at Thebes, Bay's is the only one to have the royal wholly straight axis.[61]

The overall decorative scheme seems to have closely resembled that of the tomb of Tawosret (cf. fig. 96), the first corridor opening with figures of kneeling goddesses spreading their wings, followed by a series of images of the tomb owner before various gods and also the king. Deeper in the tomb were selections from the Book of the Dead. The original constructional work in KV13 seems to have been stopped at the end of the corridor after its pillared hall. During the Twentieth Dynasty a rough extension was cut, terminating in the burial chamber of a prince Amenhirkopeshef, probably a son of Rameses VI,[62] who was interred in Tawosret's queenly sarcophagus (fig. 108).[63] Subsequently, the burial of a prince

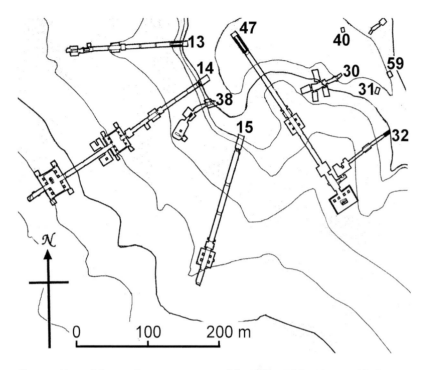

Fig. 94. Map of the southwestern corner of the Valley of the Kings, with the tombs of Sethy II (KV15), Tawosret (KV14), Bay (KV13), and Siptah (KV47); the last accidentally broke through into the adjacent KV32, apparently the tomb of the Eighteenth Dynasty queen Tiaa.

Montjuhirkopeshef, perhaps the so-named son of Rameses III, was inserted into the main corridor of the tomb.[64]

The nature of the relationship between Tawosret and Bay cannot be other than a matter of speculation, but the parallelism seen at Amada, and implicitly in the Valley of the Kings, clearly echoes that of royal consorts. There is, of course, a temptation to declare the two lovers, or even spouses, given that the queen was a widow, and Bay without a known wife: it can only be emphasized that such conclusions cannot be any more than speculation or even historical fiction. As to their relationship with their royal ward, we know nothing. However, along with the depictions already mentioned, a number of other items attest to the activities and status of Bay.

A statue of the Mnevis bull, bearing Bay's name and titles, together with a set of erased cartouches, was found in the beasts' cemetery at

Fig. 95. Entrance to the tomb of Bay (KV13).

Fig. 96. Sketch of the remains of the lintel of the entrance of the tomb of Bay. In its use of a sun disk and the goddesses Isis and Nephthys it imitates contemporary royal tombs.

Fig. 97. One of two Middle Kingdom sphinxes at Nabesha that were reinscribed by a number of later kings, including Sethy II. When Sethnakhte added his name to the monument, he erased a previous set of cartouches (almost certainly those of Siptah) and accompanying texts naming Bay.

Heliopolis.[65] Bay is also named in texts added to the bases of two Middle Kingdom sphinxes, already reinscribed with Sethy II's names, in the temple of Wadjet at Nabesha (fig. 97).[66] Bay also added texts to another ancient monument there—an offering table of Amenemhat II of the Twelfth Dynasty.[67] All these pieces reinforce the view that Bay was the key player in the running of the country.

It has been suggested[68] that a cuneiform tablet, found at Ugarit and datable to shortly before the destruction of that Levantine city,[69] refers to Bay. In it, the "Chief of the Bodyguards of the Great King of the Land of Egypt, Baya" salutes the local king, Ammurapi, in the names of Amun, Re, and Seth.[70] However, while the chancellor's correspondence with a foreign king would not be surprising, the titles are completely different from any known to have been borne by Bay, and while the similarity of the names is interesting, it seems all but certain that another individual is involved.

As for king Siptah himself, his mummy allows us to discover certain facts. As we have already seen, it suggests that his accession occurred when he had barely entered his teens, but it also shows him to have been physically disabled. Although the right leg was normal, the left leg was shortened, with much of the foot locked pointing downwards: only the king's left toes will have touched the ground when he walked (fig. 98). This has frequently been alleged to be the result of poliomyelitis, and is often cited as evidence for the disease in the ancient world, together with an Eighteenth Dynasty stela depicting a man with a similar leg and leaning on a crutch.[71] However, the same symptoms can be caused by a variety of cerebral palsy, the result of brain damage at or before birth, and this may actually be the more likely scenario, particularly as only one side seems to have been affected.

However, the theory of Egyptian monarchy was that no matter what his age or infirmity, the pharaoh was the formal ruler in whose name all acts were carried out. The earliest documented event of Siptah's reign is the installation of the new Nubian viceroy, Sethy (Q), in Year 1. The material found reused in the Serapeum, the burial place of the sacred Apis bulls at

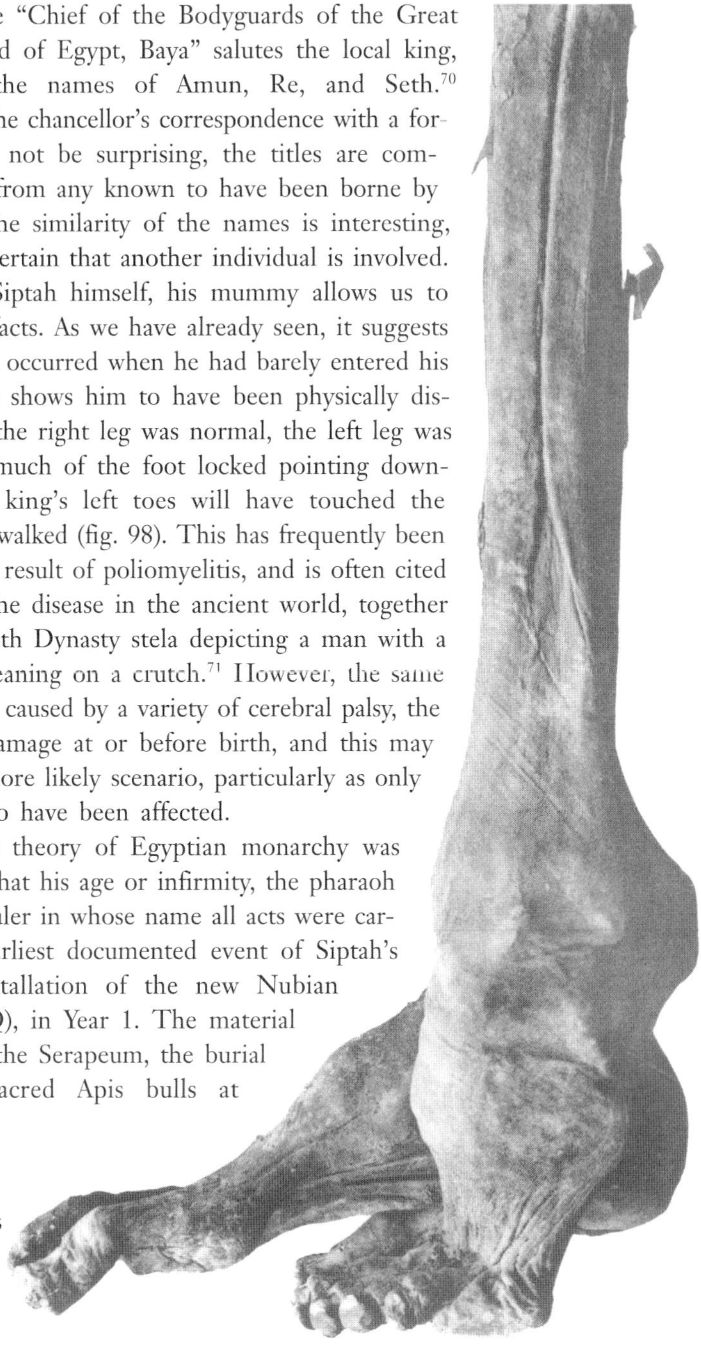

Fig. 98. The feet of the mummy of Siptah, showing his wasted and shortened left leg, probably the result of cerebral palsy.

Saqqara (p. 83), suggests that an interment took place there during the first year or so of the reign.[72]

As already noted, the first dated use of the king's later name, Akhenre Merenptah-Siptah, is in Year 3.[73] It is difficult to explain why this change took place. Of previous kings who had modified their titularies, Montjuhotep II seems to have done so to mark the progress of his campaigns of reunification, while Akhenaten was marking his change in religious outlook. In Siptah's case, it may be that some initial opposition to his accession required overcoming, at the conclusion of which a clean start, marked out by a new name, was necessary. This is, nevertheless, no more than speculation.

Sethy's period of office as viceroy was short, with his last known attestations in Year 3;[74] by Year 6 he was replaced by Hori (II), son of Kama.[75] The south temple at Buhen provides many of the documents relating to the administration of Nubia during Siptah's reign, two of which include images of the king himself (fig. 99).[76]

Officials of the realm outside Nubia were headed by the vizier Hori I, who continued in office from Sethy II's reign,[77] but are otherwise little known. Two military officers, Yuy and Anhurnakhte, are attested respectively by a stela in the Silsila rock temple[78] and by a block statue, although the latter's precise dating is not certain.[79]

Similarly, none of the major priesthoods have personnel who are firmly attested during Siptah's reign. However, Hori (IV) and Minmose were probably high priests of Amun in succession to Mahuhy,[80] while at Memphis the transition between Pahemnetjer (see above, p. 75) and Iyroy (see below, p. 117) presumably occurred under Siptah.

Indeed, very little building work is known to have taken place in the temples during Siptah's reign: the king is almost wholly absent from the national shrine at Karnak, only a single stela having been found there, east of the Sacred Lake.[81] At Ashmunein, Siptah added his names to the fecundity figures below Sethy II's reliefs in the gateway of the pylon (see above, p. 78).[82] From some temple or another in the country came a fragment of a statue.[83]

It is at Thebes-West that most of Siptah's monuments are to be found. We have already noted the usurpation of Amenmeses' stelae at the Qurna temple (pp. 57–58, 93–94) and the addition of Siptah's name in the Ramesseum (p. 83, above). Also founded there were the king's memorial temple and his tomb. The site of the memorial temple lay between the Eighteenth Dynasty monuments of Thutmose III and

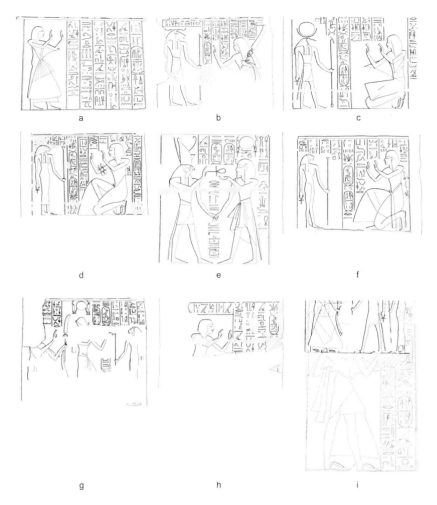

Fig. 99. Reliefs of the reign of Siptah at the South Temple at Buhen:
a. King's Envoy Neferhor (Year 1).
b. Fan-Bearer Piyay worshiping Banebdjedet (Year 3).
c. Fan-Bearer Piyay worshiping Thoth (Year 3).
d. First Charioteer Hori III worshiping Bastet (Year 3).
e. King Siptah with Horus of Buhen.
f. First Charioteer Webekhusen, son of Viceroy Hori III, worshiping Bastet (Year 6).
g. King Siptah and Fan-Bearer with Horus of Buhen
h. First Charioteer Ipy, son of Nayiba.
i. Official whose name and title is now lost, the image having been largely erased and partly over-cut by a relief of the later viceroy Ramesesnakhte (*temp*. Rameses IX).

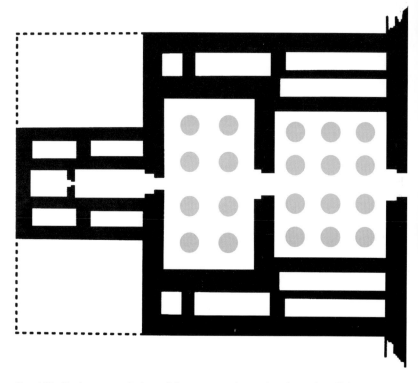

Fig. 100. Partly restored plan of the memorial temple of Siptah. All that survive are the foundation trenches.

Amenhotep II, north of the Ramesseum. Excavated by Flinders Petrie in 1896, nothing survived apart from the foundation trenches of its rear part (fig. 100).[84] A number of foundation deposits were revealed, including objects bearing the names of Siptah and—almost inevitably—the chancellor Bay (fig. 101).[85] Wine-jar dockets found on the site dating to Years 3 and 4 give an indication that work was going on in those years.[86]

Fig. 101. Sandstone foundation deposit plaque from the memorial temple of Siptah bearing the name of Bay (Petrie UC14376).

That work on the foundations was still underway at Siptah's death is suggested by the fact that one included a scarab of Tawosret as king.[87]

As noted above, the king's tomb, KV47, was commissioned on IV *prt* 21 of Year 1. The tomb[88] was cut at the same end of the Valley of the Kings as those of Sethy II and his contemporaries, but somewhat nearer the central area (fig. 94). In plan (fig. 27d), the tomb essentially followed Merenptah's prototype, and came far closer to structural completion than any of the intervening royal sepulchers, having been under construction for six years, rather than the two or three granted to the builders of KV10 and KV15. The tomb has suffered severely from flooding, the entire stone surface of the floor, walls, and ceiling beyond the pillared hall being destroyed (fig. 102); however, traces of decoration survive on the walls at either side of the entrance to the burial hall, suggesting that decorative work had at least begun in the latter.

The outer galleries (B–D) are, however, in almost perfect condition, with some very fine quality relief work. The burial hall (J) contained a granite, cartouche-form, recumbent-figure sarcophagus (fig. 103), plus vast quantities of calcite fragments. These included items belonging to the king (fig. 104),[89] but also others belonging to a queen Tiaa which have been discussed earlier (see p. 91, above).

The majority of documents from the Deir el-Medina community are prosaic in nature, but some have major historical impact. One particular example is a humble ostracon dated to III *šmw*, day 27, of Siptah's Year 5: it records that on that day "the Scribe of the Tomb, Paser, announced: 'Pharaoh, l.p.h., has killed the great enemy, Bay.'"[90]

One can only speculate what might have lain behind this elimination of the man who had dominated Egyptian politics for the past half-dozen years. Although carried out in the name of the still young Siptah, one can probably safely assume that the initiative was taken by Tawosret, signaling her intention to share power no longer with her erstwhile colleague in regency. Curiously, given this violent end to Bay's career, little attempt seems to have been made to complete his destruction by removing his name and figures from his monuments, most, if not all, of which seem to have remained intact.

From his own words ("placing the king on the seat of his father"), Bay seems to have based his promotion of Siptah upon the latter being Amenmeses' son, and it may well be that Bay's fall precipitated (or was precipitated by?) a revision of historical outlook in which Amenmeses

Fig. 102. The flood-devastated rear part of the tomb of Siptah, with the burial chamber and sarcophagus at the far end.

Fig. 103. The water-damaged burial chamber of KV47 with Siptah's sarcophagus, of typical mid-Ramesside type. All cartouches on the sarcophagus were erased and later replaced.

Fig. 104. Fragments of Siptah's canopic chest, extracted from among a large mass of alabaster fragments from KV47, which included the king's outer coffin and inner sarcophagus—together with intrusive material washed in from the breach between the tomb and KV32 (MMA 14.6.317-375).

was no longer the source of legitimacy. Thus the mutilation of the Munich statue (pp. 91–94, above) may be dated to around the downfall of Bay. How might this have reflected upon Siptah, now old enough, or nearly so, to rule untrammeled by any regency? An answer may be implicit in the fact that within eighteen months (or less) he himself was dead, and soon afterward was apparently in the process of being written out of history.

6 THE REIGN OF TAWOSRET

The last dated mention of Siptah is the Year 6 Buhen text of Webekhusen (fig. 99f). Unfortunately, no day/month is included, but it is possible that it was Siptah's burial that was recorded in the Valley of the Kings on IV *ȝḥt* 22 of an unknown year.[1] If the record is indeed his, and dates to Year 6,[2] this would place Siptah's death earlier by at least the seventy traditional days of embalming, although there are significant numbers of cases where a longer period was involved for this process.[3] Siptah would have then been dead within not much more than a year of Bay's execution.

That something sinister lay behind the young man's death is suggested by the fact that all the cartouches in the king's tomb have been erased—although later reinstated (fig. 105). Furthermore, in Tawosret's KV14, the cartouches of Siptah were replaced by those of Sethy II (fig. 90) and an original figure of her long-dead husband was incorporated into the decoration of the first pillared hall of the tomb (fig. 106).[4] Taken together, it seems that although Tawosret appears to have granted Siptah a burial, it was one that denied his status as a king,[5] and was combined with Tawosret's desire to refocus her royal affiliations on her husband, rather than the young man for whom she had ruled for half a decade.

With Siptah dead, Tawosret is now found with a full pharaonic titulary (see Appendix 3 for hieroglyphic forms):[6]

Horus	*kꜣ-nḫt mry Mꜣꜥt nb* *ꜥn m nsw mi ʾItm*	Strong bull beloved of Maat, beautiful as king like Atum
Nebti	*grg Kmt wꜥf ḫꜣswt*	Who establishes Egypt and curbs foreign lands
Golden Falcon	Unknown	
Prenomen *a*	*sꜣt Rꜥ mry ʾImn*	Daughter of Re, beloved of Amun
b⁷	*sꜣt Rꜥ [ḥnwt] tꜣ mri*	Daughter of Re, mistress of the Beloved Land
Nomen *a*	*tꜣ wsrt mr n Mwt*	Tawosret, beloved of Mut
b	*tꜣ wsrt stpt n Mwt*	Tawosret, chosen of Mut

Fig. 105. Left-hand side of the entrance to the tomb of KV47. The winged figure of the goddess Maat is accompanied by cartouches that clearly show the erasure and restoration of the king's cartouches in the tomb.

Fig. 106. Image of Sethy II on a column in the first pillared hall of KV14.

It is unclear whether the adoption of this titulary entirely postdates Siptah's death or whether a shift from regency to coregency had occurred following Bay's fall. Certainly, the construction of a new, larger, but never finished burial hall in KV14 (fig. 27e, Ka/Kb) had begun not long before Siptah's death, perhaps indicating a change in Tawosret's status.[8] The decoration of the original burial hall (J) incorporated the Book of Gates, hitherto a composition found only in the tombs of kings, rather than the Book of the Dead—not generally used for kingly sepulchers—found nearer the entrance.

A move from queen to king can definitely be seen in the oldest part of the tomb where a figure of Tawosret displays a series of modifications as her names and headgear were progressively altered from those appropriate to a queen to those of a king (fig. 107).[9] However, her transition to a fully-fledged pharaoh is made wholly explicit by the massive enlargement of the tomb that then followed. Work on the new burial hall was abandoned,[10] and instead a long corridor (K) was driven further into the hillside leading to a new, even larger burial chamber (J2).[11] Decoratively, the new corridor was adorned with the Book of Amduat, and the ultimate burial chamber with the Book of Gates.

On the other hand, in contrast to the superlative quality of the relief in the outer parts of the tomb, the extension's poor and hasty

Fig. 107. Relief of Tawosret from the left wall of the first corridor of KV14, showing the multiple reworkings of the image to reflect Tawosret's changes in status, including the change from a queen's twin plumes to a king's blue crown. The whole figure was subsequently covered in plaster and a new image of Sethnakhte carved over it, although in no case did the new carving penetrate into the original. Almost all of this plaster has now fallen away, but various clumps still survive, for example directly behind Tawosret's head, where the lower part of Sethnakhte's prenomen can be seen, partially obscuring original 𓋹 and 𓈖 signs. The king's figures were thus of considerably smaller stature than those of the queen, his chin roughly at the level of her breasts.

style shows that Tawosret was a woman in a hurry. Her queenly sarcophagus (fig. 108)[12]—ultimately reused for burying a Twentieth Dynasty prince (see p. 99, above)—was replaced by a more massive piece in typical kingly style (fig. 109).[13]

To go with her tomb, Tawosret founded a memorial temple just south of the ancient sanctuary of Thutmose IV (fig. 110). Like Siptah's, only the outline of the foundations survived to be traced by Petrie, though a new excavation under the direction of Richard Wilkinson began in 2004.[14] Foundation deposit plaques were fairly plentiful, in sandstone and faience,[15] and the presence throughout of Tawosret's kingly names, and the total lack of anything of Sethy II,[16] Siptah, or Bay indicates that the structure was founded only after the death of Siptah. A quarry-mark on a foundation block gives the date Year 7, I 3ḥt 23, presumably close to the beginning of the construction of the temple.[17] A graffito on the upper surface of the same block names the temple and gives a date in Year 8.[18] Although it may not have been wholly completed, the temple seems to have been considerably advanced prior to its subsequent dismantlement to reuse the stone.[19]

The recoverable plan shows the temple to have been fronted by a pylon, with a first court probably colonnaded on the right and left. Beyond were three rooms that should be interpreted as hypostyle halls, and the sanctuaries, including a sun-court to the north (fig. 111).

It seems that Tawosret continued the year-reckoning of Siptah, and thus some Year 6 and all Year 7 and Year 8 documents from the period should be attributed to her reign. Material from this period is scarce, and only one image of Tawosret specifically meant to represent her as a king seems to survive (fig. 112).[20]

Other attestations of the reign include foundation deposits[21] and part of an architrave from Qantir,[22] a doorjamb from Memphis,[23] another from Abydos,[24] and the usurpation of the cartouches of Siptah in the doorway of the pylon at Ashmunein (cf. p. 104, above), although with his Horus name left intact.[25] In the Sinai, various inscribed fragments have come to light at Serabit el-Khadim and Timna;[26] while beyond the frontiers of Egypt, a faience vessel bearing the names of Tawosret was found at Tell Deir Alla in Jordan,[27] and another

Fig. 108. Lid of Tawosret's queenly sarcophagus, found in Bay's KV13. It was ultimately used in prince Amenhirkopeshef D's burial, probably under Rameses VI; at this time a side-lock was carved into the original queenly wig.

as far north as Sidon on the Lebanese coast.[28] Alongside various small objects such as scarabs of uncertain provenance,[29] we know of a number of silver vessels bearing Tawosret's name deriving from a pair of hoards

Fig. 109. Upper part of the lid of the sarcophagus in KV14, ultimately reinscribed for Sethnakhte, but almost certainly originally manufactured for the kingly phase of Tawosret's career. The cartouches have certainly been recut.

Fig. 110. View of the site of the mortuary temple of Tawosret, represented by the excavation trenches in the foreground. In the background are the remains of the temple of Thutmose IV and, beyond, the Ramesseum.

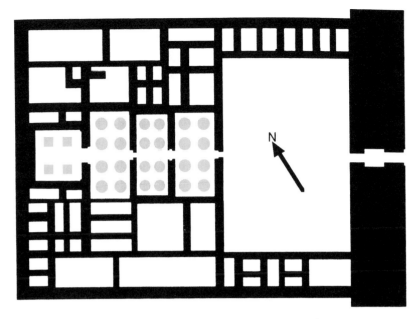

Fig. 111. Partly reconstructed plan of the memorial temple of Tawosret.

found at Tell Basta.[30] Royal names on that group went back as far as Rameses II.[31]

Concerning the officialdom of Tawosret's sole reign virtually nothing is known, although one can probably assume that most of those who served Siptah continued in office. On the other hand a statue of the high priest at Memphis, Iyroy, explicitly bears Tawosret's kingly nomen and that of Sethy II, once again indicating the way in which Tawosret as king wished to link herself explicitly with her late husband.[32] Other than the material from the memorial temple, few dated doc-uments survive, perhaps the most lengthy being a graffito

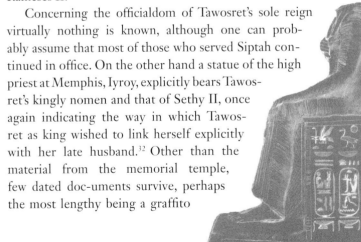

Fig. 112. Statue of Tawosret as king from Heliopolis (Medinet Nasr; Cairo, Grand Egyptian Museum.

of the scribe Thutemheb and the Chief of Medjay Nakht[min] in the temple of Thutmose III at Deir el-Bahari. This is dated to Year 7, II *šmw* 28, and explicitly mentions the memorial temple of Tawosret.[33] There is also a pair of Deir el-Medina ostraca of Year 8,[34] which seems to have been the last year of the reign—and of the dynasty.

7 DOWNFALL, RENAISSANCE, AND DECLINE

The end of the reign of Tawosret remains enveloped in a thick mist. All that is certain is that a certain Sethnakhte, a man of unknown origins but most probably a descendant of Rameses II, ultimately followed her on the throne.[1] Also, it is clear that the new king's advent was accompanied by violence. A stela from the island of Elephantine at Aswan preserves Sethnakhte's celebration of his victory (fig. 113):[2]

> The great assembly of the gods is pleased with his plans like Re, since the land had been in confusion.... [The great god] stretched out his arm and selected his person, l.p.h., from among the millions, dismissing the hundreds of thousands prior to him....
>
> Now his person, l.p.h., was like his father Sutekh, who flexed his arms to rid Egypt of those who had led it astray .... Fear of him has seized the hearts of opponents before him: they flee like [flocks] of sparrows with a falcon after them. They left silver and gold . . . which they had given to these Asiatics in order for them to bring reinforcements .... Their plans failed and the plans were futile, as every god and goddess performed wonders for the good god, proclaiming the [onse]t of a slaughter under him....

On Year 2, II *šmw* 10 there were no (more) opponents of his person, l.p.h., in any lands. They came to inform his person, l.p.h.: 'Let your heart be happy, O lord of this land; those things that the god foretold have come to pass and your foes do not exist in the land . . .'.

Here, Sethnakhte's status as a usurper is made explicit, as one whose throne was owed to divine selection as a means to rescue Egypt from chaos. Further, Egypt's parlous state is blamed on those who had "led it astray" and attempted to defend themselves from Sethnakhte's onslaught by trying to hire mercenaries from Syria-Palestine.[3]

A complementary picture of Sethnakhte's acquisition of the throne is contained in the Great Harris Papyrus, and has already been quoted in part in the previous discussion of the career of the chancellor Bay (p. 90, above). The complete passage reads as follows:

The land of Egypt had been banished, every man being a law unto himself; they had no leader for many years previously until other times when the land of Egypt was in the hands of chieftains and mayors; one killed his neighbor, whether high or low. Then another time came consisting of empty years when Irsu, a Syrian, was among them as a chieftain, having made the whole land into subjection before him; each joined with his companion in plundering their goods, and they treated the gods as they did men, and no offerings were made in the temples. But the gods then inclined themselves to peace so as to put the land in its proper state in accordance with its normal condition, and they established their son, who came forth from their flesh, as ruler of every land, upon their great throne, Userkhaure-setepenre-meryamun, Son of Re Sethnakhte-mererre-meryamun. He was Khepri-Seth when he was enraged; he set in order the entire land that had been rebellious; he killed the rebels who were in the land of Egypt. He cleansed the great throne of Egypt, being the ruler of the Two Lands on the throne of Atum.[4]

Such a lurid depiction of a benighted Egypt awaiting its savior is a common motif in Egyptian royal literature, going back at least to the Prophecy of Neferti that "foretold" the seizure of the throne by Amenemhat I at the beginning of the Twelfth Dynasty.[5] More recently, the Restoration Stela of Tutankhamun and the Edict of Horemheb had painted grim pictures of the prior state of the country as a backdrop to the kings' actions to set matters aright.[6] The propagandistic intent of both the stela and the papyrus is thus clear, with the result that neither can be regarded uncritically as a source for the state of Egypt at the time Sethnakhte appeared on the scene. The reliability of the papyrus also suffers from its having been written more than three decades after the events in question. On the other hand, it is unlikely that they are wholly falsified, and we have already seen how Bay very neatly fits the profile for the notorious "Irsu."

One issue, particularly with the papyrus account, is the time-depth being presented. In the papyrus, "Irsu" appears only after a period of anarchy: this presumably refers to the struggle between Amenmeses and Sethy II, which may well have seen the existence of areas that owed loyalty to neither king. We have already speculated (p. 72) that the reunification of the country may have been brokered in some way by Bay, and this may be the reality that lay behind the claim that Irsu "made the whole land into subjection before him." The extreme hostility expressed toward

Fig. 113. Stela of Sethnakhte from Elephantine (Elephantine Museum).

the "Syrian" and the dismissal of the time of his ascendancy as "empty years" would further suggest approval of the chancellor's execution, and the possible presence of Sethnakhte at the court of Siptah and Tawosret at that time.

But what might have caused Sethnakhte to take up arms? A clue may lie in the erased cartouches of Siptah in his tomb, whose mutilation seems to tie in with Tawosret's taking of kingly titles and the rejection of her former association with Siptah in favor of a reidentification with her late husband, Sethy II (cf. above, p. 111). These erasures were later restored, the only plausible candidate for such an act being Sethnakhte.[7] If Siptah's death was not a natural one (cf. p. 111, above), might it have been his removal that prompted Sethnakhte to rebel? Certainly his proclamation of his own kingship at the time of Siptah's death would place II *šmw* 10 of his Year 2 just over halfway through Tawosret's last known, eighth, regnal year.[8]

The alternative scenario, that the struggle began only at Tawosret's demise, would require an effective interregnum pending Sethnakhte's triumph, while also leaving the identity of his opponent wholly obscure—unless "Irsu" was *not* Bay, but some kinsman who had attempted to gain some kind of hegemony after the disappearance of the female king. There is no trace of such an individual, or evidence for an interregnum,[9] which suggests that the transition from the rump of Tawosret's regime to that of Sethnakhte was direct.

Sethnakhte adopted a titulary that harked back to that of Sethy II, actually copying his first Horus name; the Golden Falcon names also clearly allude to the means by which Sethnakhte came to the throne (see Table 3 for hieroglyphic forms):

Horus		*k3-nḫt wr pḥty*	Strong bull great of strength
Nebti		*twt ḫ'w mi T3tnn*	Image appearing like Tjatjenen
Golden Falcon	*a.*	*sḫm ḫpš dr-[rky]w.f*	Powerful of arm who drives out his rebels
	b.	*ḥwi pdt 9 'n m [nsyt]*	He who smites the Nine Bows who oppose the kingship.
Prenomen		*wsr ḫ'w R' stp n R'/mry Imn*	Appearing in power like Re, chosen of Re/beloved of Amun[10]
Nomen		*Stḫ nḫt mrr Imn(-R')*	Sethnakhte beloved of Amun (-Re)

Sethnakhte's reign following his victory was long regarded as extremely brief. However, in 2006 a stela was found at Luxor, which extended the reign from his previously attested highest date of Year 2, III *šmw* 24,[11] to some time in Year 4 (fig. 114).[12] This stela had originally been erected by Bakenkhonsu (B), high priest of Amun at Karnak,

Fig. 114. Stela of Bakenkhonsu B, dated to Year 4 of Sethnakhte, found on the sphinx avenue at Luxor.

Fig. 115. Stela of Sethnakhte in the Hathor temple at Serabit el-Khadim, dedicated by Amenopet and Sethy.

and commemorates the reerection of statues that had been displaced in some kind of disturbance—perhaps related to the conflicts that closed the Nineteenth Dynasty. There is no indication of when this Bakenkhonsu, a son of a general Amenemopet, replaced Minmose as high priest. Bakenkhonsu names Sethnakhte on one of his three known statues;[13] the remainder of his datable monuments are from the reign of Rameses III,[14] whom he served until some time before Year 26, by which time he had been replaced in office by Usermaatrenakhte.[15] On the assumption that Year 4 *was* Sethnakhte's last,[16] his death would have occurred that year on or just before Rameses III's well-attested accession day of I *šmw* 26.[17]

A smooth transition on the civil side of national administration will doubtless have been aided by the continuation in office of the vizier Hori I, of whose role in the events surrounding the transition we remain frustratingly ignorant. In Nubia, Hori II remained in office as viceroy, erecting a stela at Amara West,[18] while out in the Sinai a stela was inscribed in honor of the king by the officials Amenopet and Sethy (S) in the temple of Hathor at Serabit el-Khadim (fig. 115).[19]

Other surviving monuments of Sethnakhte's reign include the addition of the king's cartouches to monuments at Nabesha (fig. 97), Heliopolis, Memphis, and Karnak.[20] Chapel E at the Oratory of Ptah near Deir el-Medina was usurped from Amenmeses and Sethy II (see above, fig. 63), with Chapel D perhaps begun—it ultimately became a joint memorial of Sethnakhte and Rameses III (fig. 116).[21]

Sethnakhte began a tomb directly adjacent to that of Amenmeses in the Valley of the Kings (KV11: figs. 27f and 117),[22] its decoration having reached three corridors into the hillside when the tomb collided with KV10, penetrating the latter's unfinished side chamber (fig. 27b, Faa/fig. 27f, Da; fig. 118). The axis of KV11 was subsequently shifted to the right (Db), and the tomb continued. It is unclear how far the cutting of the tomb had reached at the time of Sethnakhte's death: the completed decoration down as far as the breakthrough originally bore the king's names (fig. 119), but it is likely that the actual cutting of the tomb and drafting of the decoration had proceeded considerably further, perhaps as far as the pillared hall (F).[23]

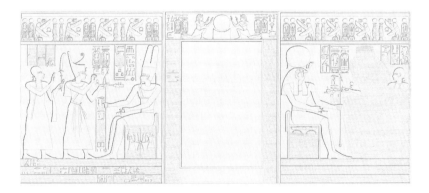

Fig. 116. Rear wall of Chapel D in the Oratory of Ptah near Deir el-Medina, completed by Rameses III as a joint memorial to himself and his father.

Fig. 117. The outer part of KV11, begun by Sethnakhte, showing the entrances to the side chambers that are unique to this sepulcher.

Fig. 118. Corridor Da in tomb KV11, showing how the cutting of such tombs began at ceiling level, descending in steps. At the bottom can be seen where Sethnakhte's quarrymen accidentally broke through into part of the adjacent tomb of Amenmeses (KV10).

Fig. 119. Image of Sethnakhte in the outer part of KV11, with the cartouches later plastered over and the names of Rameses III surcharged.

However, the tomb was far from being ready for an interment at Sethnakhte's demise, and the tomb of Tawosret was therefore appropriated for this. It seems likely that the necessary changes were carried out during the period of embalmment, as they show every indication of haste. In the outer corridor of the tomb, each of the much-altered figures of the queen was overlaid by plaster and an image of the king carved and painted over the top. To make room for his cartouches and titulary, however, these secondary figures were of considerably smaller stature than those of Tawosret. Most of this plaster has now fallen away, leaving in some cases hybrid images with two sets of arms at different levels (cf. fig. 107)! However, as the workmen moved deeper into the tomb, the pressure of time clearly made itself felt, as few other figures underwent this comprehensive reworking: most of the remaining figures of Tawosret were simply covered with plaster, and only Sethnakhte's names and titles were drawn in black on the unpainted plaster. Occasionally, the king's actual figure was sketched in outline (figs. 120–21); the cartouches of Sethy II/Siptah were simply plastered over and surcharged in ink. The names on the sarcophagus were erased and recut (figs. 109 and 122).

Fig. 120. Rear wall of chamber E in KV14, showing the replacement of Tawosret's images with the names of Sethnakhte.

It may be assumed that Tawosret had never been buried in the tomb: her fate remains completely obscure, although no intentional mutilation of her names seems to have been recorded on any of her memorials.[24] Indeed, under Rameses VI we have a mention of Tawosret with a cartouche,[25] which suggests that she did not receive the degree of posthumous opprobrium reserved for the likes of Akhenaten and Amenmeses. She also survives into the fourth-century BC history of Manetho under the name "Thuôris," albeit transmogrified into a man, a legendary king of Thebes[26] "who in Homer is called Polybius, husband of Alcandra, and in whose time Troy was taken."[27]

Nothing is known of any memorial temple of Sethnakhte, although a cult was certainly maintained at Abydos,[28] with the king also commemorated at Deir el-Medina (see above, fig. 63). The inner coffin of Sethnakhte eventually made its way to

Fig. 121. Pillar in KV14 with an inked outline of Sethnakhte. These pillars are among the few places in the tomb where more than his simple names replaced Tawosret's image and names.

Fig. 122. Lid of the sarcophagus in KV14, usurped by Sethnakhte with the rest of tomb. It is shown as found, lying on its side after being tipped off the coffer by robbers; most of the walls of the coffer were demolished in antiquity. The sarcophagus has now been restored.

KV35,²⁹ but nothing is known with certainty of the fate of his mummy—the trough of the coffin held the mummy of Merenptah and the upturned lid that of an unidentified woman.³⁰

Sethnakhte's death marked the accession of his son Rameses III and the opening of the last phase of the history of the New Kingdom.³¹ The early years of the new reign were dominated by renewed conflict with Merenptah's old foes, the Libyans and the Sea Peoples: in Year 5 the former made a new advance on the western Delta. In the battle that followed, Rameses' forces were victorious, thus temporarily securing the western frontier.

The second and far more serious crisis came three years later when the Sea Peoples, having now apparently brought about the downfall of the key regimes of the Levant—including even that of the Hittites—approached the eastern border of Egypt by land and sea. Once again, Rameses was successful in defeating the enemy, and much of the decoration of his great memorial temple was dedicated to his victory (fig. 123–24).³²

Year 11 saw yet another invasion from Libya. Again the enemy was driven back, over two thousand men were killed, and the captured leaders executed. Nevertheless, the Libyan population of the western Delta continued to increase by peaceful infiltration and would later form the basis for a line of chieftains that would ultimately take the throne of Egypt.³³

In his graphic commemoration of his victories, Rameses III was clearly imitating Rameses II, and also attempting to follow him in the extensive building program that was initiated. Indeed, throughout the reign, the third Rameses' debt to his ancestor is explicit. Not only were the king's names modeled on those of Rameses II, but also the names of his children were directly taken from those of the old king.³⁴ Rameses III also

Fig. 123. North wall of the Great Temple at Medinet Habu, the principal canvas for the commemoration of Rameses III's victory over the Sea Peoples.

Fig. 124. Detail of Rameses III's sea battle from the north wall of Medinet Habu.

Fig. 125. The Min Festival as depicted in the Great Temple at Medinet Habu. The statues of former kings shown to the right reflect the "official" view of the Nineteenth Dynasty: the figures begin with Rameses III, followed in turn by Sethnakhte, Sethy II, Merenptah, Rameses II, Sethy I, and Rameses I. The following images of Horemheb and Amenhotep III also reflect a redacted view of history, excluding the "heretic" kings Akhenaten, Tutankhamun, and Ay, of the late Eighteenth Dynasty.

imitated the second Rameses by taking multiple Great Wives. In doing so, he seems to have sown the seeds of his own downfall.

By the late twenties of the reign, economic problems were becoming manifest, made most visible in failures to pay the Deir el-Medina workmen, which led to a sit-down strike in year 29.[35] Against this background was hatched a plot against the king's life, executed in Year 32, apparently with the aim of placing one wife's offspring on the throne in place of the acknowledged heir, born of another wife:[36] the poisoned legacy of Rameses II had not been quenched by the events of the close of the Nineteenth Dynasty.

The renaissance represented by the reign of Rameses III was followed by a slow but steady decline under his successors, beginning with Rameses IV.[37] On more than one occasion the conventional father-son succession of the kingship was frustrated by skulduggery, accident, or disease,[38] while marauders infiltrated from the western desert in the Thebaid. Furthermore, economic decline was manifested by disorder and the plundering of the Theban necropolis, as attested by judicial records from the reigns of Rameses IX and XI (fig. 126).[39]

By the end of the dynasty the integrity of the state was breaking down, with a period of disorder that included the "suppression" of the Theban high priest Amenhotep G (cf. fig. 127),[40] and finally a war in

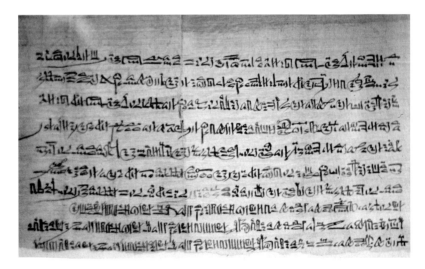

Fig. 126 Papyrus Leopold II, part of one of the key records of the tomb robbery trials of the reign of Rameses IX (Brussels E6857).

Fig. 127. The "Wall of the High Priest" at Karnak, carved by the high priest of Amun, Amenhotep G, and showing the pontiff on the same scale as Rameses IX. Amenhotep's "suppression" was one manifestation of the troubles that marked the last decades of the New Kingdom.

Nubia that seems ultimately to have resulted in the loss of that territory and its resources by the Egyptian state.[41] Egyptian power and prestige evaporated also in the Levant: the Report of Wenamun form the last decade of the dynasty paints a sorry picture of how this emissary of the king of Egypt was treated by the ruler of Byblos, who had once been the pharaoh's unquestioning tributary.[42] Indeed, it has been suggested that from the middle years of Rameses IX's reign the kingship itself fractured, with Rameses IX and X reigning in part contemporaneously with Rameses XI,[43] in many ways anticipating the kinds of divisions that typified the latter part of the Third Intermediate Period.

While one cannot, of course, directly attribute this dissolution of the empire of the New Kingdom to the late Nineteenth Dynasty's family feuds and the violent close of the reign of Rameses III, those events clearly contributed to the malaise that pervaded the last decades of the Twentieth Dynasty. Most ironically of all, the ultimate beneficiaries of the decline of the Ramesside royal house were Merenptah's erstwhile foes, the Libyans, whose names would soon emerge on the throne of the pharaohs in the form of the Shoshenqs, Takelots, and Osorkons who were to dominate much of the coming Third Intermediate Period.

APPENDICES

Appendix 1

Chronology of ancient Egypt

LE = Lower Egypt only; UE = Upper Egypt.
All New Kingdom and Third Intermediate Period dates are based on the scheme set out in Dodson 2012: 181-89; in any case all dates are more or less conjectural prior to 690 BC. Parentheses indicate a co-ruler.

Early Dynastic Period

Dynasty 1	3050–2810 BC
Dynasty 2	2810–2660

Old Kingdom

Dynasty 3	2660–2600
Dynasty 4	2600–2470
Dynasty 5	2470–2360
Dynasty 6	2360–2195

First Intermediate Period

Dynasties 7/8	2195–2160
Dynasties 9/10 (LE)	2160–2040
Dynasty 11a (UE)	2160–2065

Middle Kingdom

Dynasty 11b	2065–1994
Dynasty 12	1994–1780
Dynasty 13	1780–1650

Second Intermediate Period

Dynasty 14 (LE)	1700–1650
Dynasty 15 (LE)	1650–1535
Dynasty 16 (UE)	1650–1590
Dynasty 17 (UE)	1585–1540

New Kingdom

Dynasty 18	1540–1278	
Ahmose I		1540–1516
Amenhotep I		1516–1496
Thutmose I		1496–1481
Thutmose II		1481–1468
Thutmose III		1468–1415
(Hatshepsut		1462–1447)
Amenhotep II		1415–1386
Thutmose IV		1386–1377
Amenhotep III		1377–1337
Amenhotep IV/Akhenaten		1337–1321
(Smenkhkare		1325–1323)
(Neferneferuaten		1322–1319)
Tutankhaten/amun		1321–1312
Ay		1312–1308
Horemheb		1308–1278
Dynasty 19	1291–1188	
Rameses I		1278–1276
Sethy I		1276–1265
Rameses II		1265–1200
Merenptah		1200–1190
Sethy II		1190–1185
(Amenmeses		1190–1187)
Siptah		1185–1179
Tawosret		1179–1177
Dynasty 20	1179–1078	
Sethnakhte		1179–1175
Rameses III		1175–1142
Rameses IV		1142–1136
Rameses V		1136–1132
Rameses VI		1132–1125
Rameses VII		1125–1118

Rameses VIII	1118–1116
Rameses IX	1116–1098
Rameses X	1098–1095
Rameses XI	1110–1095
	(LE) + 1095–1078

Third Intermediate Period

Dynasty 21	1078–941
Dynasty 22	943–736
Dynasty 23 (UE)	736–666
Dynasty 24 (LE)	734–721
Dynasty 25	745–656

Saite Period

Dynasty 26	664–525

Late Period

Dynasty 27 (Persians)	525–405
Dynasty 28	404–399
Dynasty 29	399–380
Dynasty 30	380–339
Dynasty 31 (Persians)	339–332

Hellenistic Period

Dynasty of Macedonia	332–310
Dynasty of Ptolemy	310–30

Roman Period — BC 30–395 AD

Appendix 2

Correlation of the reigns from the end of the reign of Merenptah to the beginning of the reign of Rameses III

Year BC	Season	Month	Merenptah	Sethy II	Amenmeses	Siptah	Tawosret	Sethnakhte
1191	ȝḥt	III						
1191	ȝḥt	IV						
1191	prt	I	10					
1191	prt	II						
1191	prt	III						
1190	prt	IV						
1190	šmw	I						
1190	šmw	II						
1190	šmw	III						
1190	šmw	IV						
1190	ȝḥt	I		1				
1190	ȝḥt	II						
1190	ȝḥt	III						
1190	ȝḥt	IV			1			
1190	prt	I						
1190	prt	II						
1190	prt	III						
1189	prt	IV						
1189	šmw	I						
1189	šmw	II						
1189	šmw	III						
1189	šmw	IV						
1189	ȝḥt	I		2				
1189	ȝḥt	II						
1189	ȝḥt	III						
1189	ȝḥt	IV			2			
1189	prt	I						
1189	prt	II						
1189	prt	III						
1188	prt	IV						
1188	šmw	I						
1188	šmw	II						
1188	šmw	III						
1188	šmw	IV						
1188	ȝḥt	I		[3]				
1188	ȝḥt	II						
1188	ȝḥt	III						
1188	ȝḥt	IV			3			
1188	prt	I						
1188	prt	II						
1188	prt	III						
1187	prt	IV						
1187	šmw	I						
1187	šmw	II						
1187	šmw	III						
1187	šmw	IV						
1187	ȝḥt	I		[4]				
1187	ȝḥt	II						
1187	ȝḥt	III						
1187	ȝḥt	IV			4			
1187	prt	I						
1187	prt	II						

Year BC	Season	Month	Sethy II	Amenmeses	Siptah	Tawosret	Sethnakhte
1187	prt	III					
1186	prt	IV	[5]	4			
1186	šmw	I					
1186	šmw	II					
1186	šmw	III					
1186	šmw	IV					
1186	ȝḥt	I	5				
1186	ȝḥt	II					
1186	ȝḥt	III					
1186	ȝḥt	IV					
1186	prt	I					
1186	prt	II					
1186	prt	III					
1185	prt	IV					
1185	šmw	I					
1185	šmw	II					
1185	šmw	III	6				
1185	šmw	IV					
1185	ȝḥt	I					
1185	ȝḥt	II					
1185	ȝḥt	III					
1185	ȝḥt	IV					
1185	prt	I					
1185	prt	II					
1185	prt	III					
1184	prt	IV					
1184	šmw	I					
1184	šmw	II					
1184	šmw	III					
1184	šmw	IV					
1184	ȝḥt	I			1		
1184	ȝḥt	II					
1184	ȝḥt	III					
1184	ȝḥt	IV					
1184	prt	I					
1184	prt	II					
1184	prt	III					
1183	prt	IV					
1183	šmw	I					
1183	šmw	II					
1183	šmw	III					
1183	šmw	IV					
1183	ȝḥt	I			2		
1183	ȝḥt	II					
1183	ȝḥt	III					
1183	ȝḥt	IV					
1183	prt	I					
1183	prt	II					
1183	prt	III					
1182	prt	IV			3		
1182	šmw	I					
1182	šmw	II					

Reigns/Regnal Years

Year BC	Season	Month	Sethy II	Amenmeses	Siptah	Tawosret	Sethnakhte
1182	šmw	III					
1182	šmw	IV					
1182	ꜣḫt	I			3		
1182	ꜣḫt	II					
1182	ꜣḫt	III					
1182	ꜣḫt	IV					
1182	prt	I					
1182	prt	II					
1182	prt	III					
1181	prt	IV					
1181	šmw	I					
1181	šmw	II			4		
1181	šmw	III					
1181	šmw	IV					
1181	ꜣḫt	I					
1181	ꜣḫt	II					
1181	ꜣḫt	III					
1181	ꜣḫt	IV					
1181	prt	I					
1181	prt	II					
1181	prt	III					
1180	prt	IV					
1180	šmw	I					
1180	šmw	II			5		
1180	šmw	III					
1180	šmw	IV					
1180	ꜣḫt	I					
1180	ꜣḫt	II					
1180	ꜣḫt	III					
1180	ꜣḫt	IV					
1180	prt	I					
1180	prt	II					
1180	prt	III					
1179	prt	IV					
1179	šmw	I			6		
1179	šmw	II					
1179	šmw	III					
1179	šmw	IV					
1179	ꜣḫt	I					
1179	ꜣḫt	II					
1179	ꜣḫt	III				6	
1179	ꜣḫt	IV					
1179	prt	I					
1179	prt	II					
1179	prt	III					
1178	prt	IV				1	
1178	šmw	I					
1178	šmw	II			7		
1178	šmw	III					
1178	šmw	IV					
1178	ꜣḫt	I					
1178	ꜣḫt	II					
1178	ꜣḫt	III					
1178	ꜣḫt	IV			8	2	
1178	prt	I					

Reigns/Regnal Years

Year BC	Season	Month	Sethy II	Amenmeses	Siptah	Tawosret	Sethnakhte	Rameses III
1178	prt	II						
1178	prt	III				8		
1177	prt	IV						
1177	šmw	I					2	
1177	šmw	II						
1177	šmw	III						
1177	šmw	IV						
1177	ꜣḫt	I						
1177	ꜣḫt	II						
1177	ꜣḫt	III						
1177	ꜣḫt	IV						
1177	prt	I						
1177	prt	II						
1177	prt	III						
1176	prt	IV					3	
1176	šmw	I						
1176	šmw	II						
1176	šmw	III						
1176	šmw	IV						
1176	ꜣḫt	I						
1176	ꜣḫt	II						
1176	ꜣḫt	III						
1176	ꜣḫt	IV						
1176	prt	I						
1176	prt	II					4	
1176	prt	III						
1175	prt	IV						
1175	šmw	I						
1175	šmw	II						
1175	šmw	III						
1175	šmw	IV						
1175	ꜣḫt	I						
1175	ꜣḫt	II						
1175	ꜣḫt	III						1
1175	ꜣḫt	IV						
1175	prt	I						
1175	prt	II						
1175	prt	III						
1174	prt	IV						
1174	šmw	I						
1174	šmw	II						
1174	šmw	III						
1174	šmw	IV						
1174	ꜣḫt	I						
1174	ꜣḫt	II						
1174	ꜣḫt	III						2
1174	ꜣḫt	IV						
1174	prt	I						
1174	prt	II						
1174	prt	III						
1173	prt	IV						
1173	šmw	I						
1173	šmw	II						
1173	šmw	III						3
1173	šmw	IV						

Appendix 3

Royal names of the late Nineteenth Dynasty

Key: H. = Horus name;
    Nb. = Nebti name;
    G. = Golden Falcon name;
    P. = Prenomen;
    N. = Nomen

Sethy II

H.a		*kȝ-nḫt wr pḥty*
b		*kȝ-nḫt mry Rꜥ*
c		*kȝ-nḫt mk Kmt*
Nb.a		*nḫt ḫpš dr pḏt 9*
b		*sḫm ḫpš dr pḏt 9*
c		*mk Kmt wꜥf ḫȝswt*
G.a		*ꜥȝ nrw m tȝw nbw*
b		*ꜥȝ nḫtw m tȝw nbw*
P.		*wsr-ḫprw-Rꜥ stp n Rꜥ*
		wsr ḫprw Rꜥ mry ꞽmn
N.		*Stḫy mr n Ptḥ*

Amenmeses

H.		*kȝ-nḫt mry Mȝꜥt smn tȝwy nb ḥbw sd mꞽ Tȝṯnn*
Nb.		*wr bꞽȝwt m ꞽpt-swt*
G.		*ꜥȝ ḫpš sȝ Wȝst n ms.sw*
P.		*mn mꞽ Rꜥ stp n Rꜥ*
		mn mꞽ Rꜥ stp n Rꜥ mry ꞽmn
N.		*ꞽmn(-Rꜥ) mss ḥqȝ Wȝst*

Siptah (Years 1/2)

H.		*kȝ-nḫt mry Ḥꜥpꞽ sꜥnḫ tȝ nb m kȝ.f rꜥ nb*
P.		*sḫꜥ n Rꜥ mry ꞽmn / stp n Rꜥ*
N.		*Rꜥ mss sȝ Ptḥ*

Siptah (Years 2–6)

H.*a* k3-nḫt mry Ḥʿpi sʿnḫ t3 nb m k3.f rʿ nb

  b k3-nḫt mr T3tnn

  c k3-nḫt wr pḥti mì 'Imn

  d ḥʿ m 3ḫ-bit

Nb. sʿ3 'Iwnw

G. [...] mì ìt.f Rʿ

P. 3ḫ n R stp n Rʿ

N. mr n Ptḥ s3 Ptḥ

Tawosret

H. k3-nḫt mry M3ʿt nb ʿn m nsw mì 'Itm

Nb. grg Kmt wʿf ḫ3swt

P.*a* s3t Rʿ mry 'Imn

  b s3t-Rʿ [ḥnwt] t3 mrì

N.*a* t3 wsrt mr n Mwt

  b t3 wsrt stpt n Mwt

Sethnakhte

H. k3-nḫt wr pḥty

Nb. twt ḥʿw mì T3tnn

G.*a* sḫm ḫpš dr-[rk] yw.f

  b ḥwì pdt 9 ʿn m [nsyt]

P.*a* wsr ḫʿw Rʿ stp n Rʿ

  b wsr ḫʿw Rʿ mry 'Imn

  c wsr ḫʿw Rʿ stp n Rʿ mry 'Imn

N. Stḫ nḫt mrr 'Imn-Rʿ

Appendix 4

Tentative genealogy of the late Nineteenth Dynasty

Sethy

RAMESE

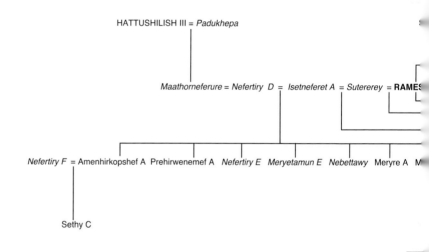

HATTUSHILISH III = *Padukhepa*

Maathorneferure = *Nefertiry D* = *Isetneferet A* = *Sutererey* = RAMES

Nefertiry F = Amenhirkopshef A   Prehirwenemef A   *Nefertiry E*   *Meryetamun E*   *Nebettawy*   Meryre A   M

Sethy C

Hori I

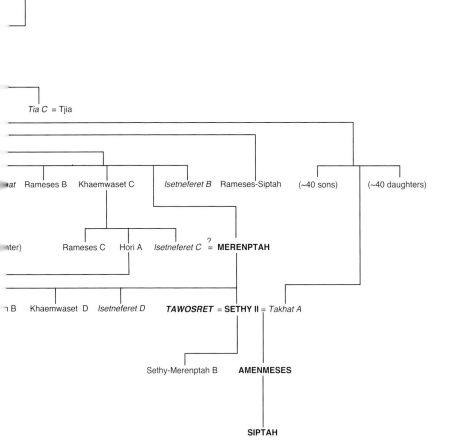

set B = *Taemwadjy*

uia = *Raia*

Tia C = Tjia

at   Rameses B   Khaemwaset C   *Isetneferet B*   Rameses-Siptah   (~40 sons)   (~40 daughters)

ater)   Rameses C   Hori A   *Isetneferet C* $\overset{?}{=}$ **MERENPTAH**

ι B   Khaemwaset D   *Isetneferet D*   ***TAWOSRET*** = **SETHY II** = *Takhat A*

Sethy-Merenptah B   **AMENMESES**

SIPTAH

NOTES

Abbreviations and Conventions

1 Cf. Dodson 2000b on some general issues and p. 131, below, for a potential adjustment that would demand something like a two-decade reduction in dates for the period under discussion in this book as expressed in terms of years BC. For a comprehensive discussion embodying the latest consensus on Egyptian chronology and its limitations, see Horung, Krauss, and Warburton, eds. 2006.

Introduction: The Glory Years

1 Dodson 2009a: 126–28.

2 Cairo JE44863–4: Porter and Moss 1972: 188; Delvaux 1992.

3 It has been suggested that this man is also named on stela Chicago OI 11456 (Cruz-Uribe 1978; for doubts see van Dijk in Martin 1997: 61 n. 4); for the use of letters to distinguish homonyms, see pp. xxi–xxii, above.

4 Cf. Brand 2000: 333–43.

5 See Dodson 2009a: 43–52, 65–67.

6 Cairo JE60539 (the "Year 400 Stela"—Porter and Moss 1934: 23; Kitchen 1968–90: II, 287–88); on this and Paramessu's broader family background, see Gaballa and Kitchen 1968, Goedicke 1981, van Dijk in Martin 1997: 60–62, Kitchen 1993ff(b): II, 168–72; Brand 2000: 336–43 and Fisher 2001: I, 7–9.

7 The remains of a miniature obelisk (Edinburgh NMS A.1965.318) bears on two faces the names of Horemheb and on the third that of Rameses I (Aldred 1968: 100–102).

8 Louvre C57 (Kitchen 1968–90: 2–3).

9 KV16: the burial chamber was cut at the point where the second corridor should have begun (Porter and Moss 1960–64: 534–35; Thomas 1966: 103–104).

10 Brand 2000: 310–12.

11 See Brand 2000: 305–309.

12 Brand 2000: 119–299.

13 Brand 2000: 45–118.
14 Some have argued that the lady in question was the widow of Akhenaten; cf. however, works cited in next note.
15 Murnane 1990: 1–38; Dodson 2009a: 89–94.
16 For Sethy's foreign policy, see Murnane 1990.
17 Porter and Moss 1939: 25; cf. Fisher 2001: I, 9–11.
18 Brand 2000: 312–32.
19 See n. 11, above.
20 Kitchen 1968–90: II, 323–36.
21 Cf. Brand 2000: 34–36.
22 Porter and Moss 1952: 23–24; Kitchen 1968–90: II, 198–99.
23 Fisher 2001: I, 43–70. His name was changed to Amenhirkopeshef (A) soon afterward.
24 Gomaà 1973; Fisher 2001: I, 89–05.
25 Replacing the figure of a senior army officer named Mehy (see Murnane 1990: 107–14).
26 Cf. Kitchen 1982a: 102; Fisher 2001: I, pl. 99–100.
27 Porter and Moss 1968–90: II, 858–68; Fisher 2001: I, 33–42.
28 Porter and Moss 1960–64: 298–99; Epigraphic Survey 1980: pl. 47, 57.
29 Porter and Moss 1974–81: 327, 332.
30 Cf. Ikram 1989: 100–101.
31 Cairo JE59873 (Porter and Moss 1960–64: 774); the couple's two sons are never shown in such contexts (cf. Dodson 2009a: 6, 13–16).
32 Kitchen 1968–90: II, 848–53, 928; Schmidt and Willeitner 1997.
33 Porter and Moss 1952: 100.
34 Porter and Moss 1952: 111–13.
35 Sourouzian 1989: 2–5.
36 Porter and Moss 1937: 210.
37 On the question of Henutmire's parentage, cf. Dodson 2002: 271, *contra* Sourouzian 1983, who would make Henutmire a daughter of Rameses II himself. Cf. also n. 47 below.
38 There is no evidence that the two Great Wives attested alongside Thutmose IV were contemporary with one another, while the attribution of the *ḥmt-nsw-wrt* title to Iset A (wife of Thutmose II), Tiaa (Amenhotep II) and Mutemwia (Thutmose IV) seems to date to their sons' reigns.
39 The doubts that have been expressed about Sitamun's parentage have apparently been resolved by the confirmation that a princess of the name appears in the reliefs at Soleb (Schiff Giorgini 1998–2003: V, pl. 97).
40 Cf. Dodson 2009b.
41 Heir from the beginning of the reign until somewhere between Year 21 and Year 35 (Fisher 2001: I, 70).
42 Heir from Amenhirkopeshef's death until the early 50s of the reign (Fisher 2001: 78–79).
43 Briefly heir up to Year 55 (cf. Fisher 2001: 99).
44 E.g. Fisher 2001: pl. 105–07; Porter and Moss 1934: 16; 1972: 311–12.
45 E.g. Fisher 2001: pl. 128–32.

46 E.g. Porter and Moss 1934: 16; 1972: 311–12.
47 Vatican 22678 (Porter and Moss 1952: 413); if Henutmire were rather a younger daughter of Rameses II (cf. sources quoted in n. 37, above) it is difficult to see why she should be depicted on this statue of her grandmother, probably dead before Henutmire was even born.
48 Fisher 2001: I, 99–105 (Khaemwaset); 117–18 (Meryatum).
49 Cf. Schulman 1986.
50 Kitchen 1993ff(b): II, 3–54.
51 Kitchen 1968–90: II, 225–32.
52 Habachi et al. 2001.
53 Sourouzian 1989: 16; Fisher 2001: I, 112
54 Using the designations set out in Dodson 2004.
55 Louvre N412 (Porter and Moss 1974–81: 784; Sourouzian 1989: 17–18.
56 Florence 1681 (Sourouzian 1989: 18–19).
57 Kitchen 1968–90: II, 145; Wente 1980: 261; Sourouzian 1989: 16, 18–19; the block in question is presently lost, and it is not clear whether the Merenptah label is original on a very late redaction of the Qadesh tableaux, or a later addition, usurping a figure of the twelfth son, Horhirwenemef.
58 Bakry 1971a: 1–8; Sourouzian 1989: 24–25.
59 Peden 1994; cf. Hornung 2006: 212.

Chapter 1: The Reign of Merenptah

1 Cf. Sourouzian 1989: 17, 20.
2 Kitchen 1968–90: II, 865; Fisher 2001: I, pl. 32B, 33A, 37A.
3 Interestingly, Merenptah's nomen is always written with a figure of the god Ptah, never with the god's name spelled out (cf. fig. 47).
4 For Merenptah's full titulary, see von Beckerath 1999: 156–59; the erosion of the status of the Horus, Nebti, and Golden Falcon names begins under the Thutmoside kings and only reverts to earlier patterns late in the Third Intermediate Period.
5 Cruz-Uribe 1977; cf., however, Sourouzian 1989: 27–28 n.128.
6 Porter and Moss 1937: 209, 212; Kitchen 1968–90: IV, 73–74, 89–90; Sourouzian 1989: 198.
7 Porter and Moss 1937: 217; Sourouzian 1989: 193.
8 Sourouzian 1989: 160–61.
9 Luxor Museum J131 (Sourouzian 1989: 160–61). The fact that the other statue's representation of Isetneferet omits the title "King's Sister" found in Bintanat's label-text is a factor that argues against Isetneferet C also having been a sister of Merenptah.
10 Cf. Eaton-Krauss 1981.
11 BM EA68682; it is also possible that this could be a figure of Merenptah himself while crown prince (Kitchen 1968–90: VII, 220; Malek 1999: 638).
12 Cairo JE37481 (Porter and Moss 1934: 20; Kitchen 1968–90: IV, 43; VII, 220; Sourouzian 1989: 83–85[39], pl. 16) and Cairo JE37483, from Tanis (Porter and Moss 1934: 17; Kitchen 1968–90: IV, 43; VII, 220; Sourouzian 1989: 79–82[38], pl. 15); fragmentary example from Tell Basta (Porter and Moss 1934: 30;

Sourouzian 1989: 66[23]—Gauthier 1914: 126[LV D] states that the piece is in Cairo "sous le n° 702"; however, this Exhibition Number actually refers to CG1240); Cairo JE35126, from Ashmunein (ex-Rameses II, Porter and Moss 1934: 167; Kitchen 1968–90: IV, 58–59; Sourouzian 1989: 117–20[65a]); Cairo CG1240, perhaps from Medinet Habu (Porter and Moss 1960: 775; Kitchen 1968–90: IV, 66–67; Sourouzian 1989: 172–74.

13 Porter and Moss 1937: 210; 217; Sourouzian 1989: 198.

14 Porter and Moss 1972: 132–3[491–495]; Sourouzian 1986: 145–9; Yurko 1978; Yurco 1986; Brand 2009a. The prince was once misidentified as Rameses II's son Sethy B when it was believed that the reliefs themselves belonged to Rameses (Yurco 1986: 201–205). The prince's name has been mutilated, presumably at the same time as those of Merenptah himself were erased: cf. below p. 43.

15 pBM EA10183 (Kitchen 1968–90: IV, 82).

16 Cairo TR 16/2/25/8 (Kitchen 1968–90: II, 900; Fisher 2001: I, 109–10; II, 151–54, attributed to Sethy B, ninth son of Rameses II); this, however, omits the "Merenptah" element from the name, but may be attributed to Sethy-Merenptah A on the basis of the use of the "Noble" title (not otherwise attested for Sethy B) and the fact that his father's cartouches have been erased on this piece—something not generally found on Rameses II's monuments, but not uncommon on Merenptah's (Brand 2009).

17 Once confounded with Khaemwaset C, son of Rameses II: Yurco 1986: 205–206 and Brand 2009.

18 Sourouzian 1989: 27–28, n. 128.

19 Sourouzian 1989: 22–24.

20 Cairo JE37465; Berlin ÄM7625 (Porter and Moss 1934: 18).

21 Kitchen 1968–90: IV, 26.

22 Oren (ed.) 2000.

23 Manassa 2003: 25–27.

24 Porter and Moss 1972: 131; Kitchen 1968–90: 2–12; Sourouzian: 143–49.

25 Yurco 1986; Kitchen 1993ff(b): II, 72–78; Brand 2011.

26 Cairo CG34025 (Porter and Moss 1972: 448); Sourouzian 1989: 167–70.

27 Porter and Moss 1972: 131; Kitchen 1968–90: IV, 12–19; Sourouzian 1989: 144–45.

28 The naming of Israel on the stela is the source of its modern name, the "Israel Stela," in spite of the vast majority of the text being about the Libyan war.

29 Cf. Sourouzian 1989: 209–15.

30 Cf. Bryce 1998: 364–65.

31 Kitchen 1968–90: 1–2, 33–37.

32 E.g. from Alexandria, Abukir, and San el-Hagar (Tanis; Sourouzian 1989: 75–101).

33 Dismantled from early in the Third Intermediate Period onwards: cf. Uphill 1984; Habachi 2001: 112–13, 115.

34 Sourouzian 1989: 102–03.

35 Sourouzian 1989: 55–74.

36 Porter and Moss 1974–81: 854–61; Sourouzian 1989: 33–50; O'Connor 1991.

37 Statue Cairo JE66571 (Kitchen 1968–90: IV, 56[26A]; Sourouzian 1989: 107).

38 Six Twelfth Dynasty columns, including BM EA1123, MFA 91.259 and UPMAA E.636; a statue of Senwosret III, Cairo JE45976 (Porter and Moss 1934: 118–21; Sourouzian 1989: 109–10).

39 Porter and Moss 1934: 126–27; Kitchen 1968–90: IV, 56–58; Sourouzian 1989: 111–15.

40 Porter and Moss 1934: 175–76; Sourouzian 1989: 122.

41 Cairo JE35126 (Porter and Moss 1934: 167; Kitchen 1968–90: IV, 58–59; Sourouzian 1989: 117–22).

42 Porter and Moss 1939: 29–30; Sourouzian 1989: 125–28.

43 Including Cairo CG557 (Kitchen 1968–90: IV, 59–62; Sourouzian 1989: 129–35).

44 Cairo JE46068 (Porter and Moss 1939: 106; Sourouzian 1989: 137–39).

45 Kitchen 1968–90: IV, 52; Sourouzian 1989: 139–40.

46 Including statues Cairo CG41148 and BM EA61 (Porter and Moss 1972: 75; 142, 288; Sourouzian 1989: 150–53).

47 Sourouzian 1989: 154–57.

48 Kitchen 1968–90: IV, 63–64; Sourouzian 1989: 157–62.

49 Porter and Moss 1972: 447–49; Sourouzian 1989: 162–74; Jaritz 1992, 2001; Jaritz, Dominicus and Sourouzian 1995; Jaritz et al. 1996, 1999 and 2001; Bickel 1997; Dominicus 2004.

50 Cairo JE67379; MFA 38.1395; Worcester, MA, 1971–28; two in New York, Institute of Art and Archaeology, NN (Kitchen 1968–90: IV, 72–73; Sourouzian 1989: 189–90).

51 Kitchen 1968–90: IV, 76; Sourouzian 1989: 191, 199–200.

52 Porter and Moss 1937: 208–13; Kitchen 1968–90: IV, 73–74, 89–91, 147; Klemm 1988: 41–45; Sourouzian 1989: 197–99; Thiem 2000.

53 Porter and Moss 1937: 217; Kitchen 1968–90: IV, 74–76; Sourouzian 1989: 197–97.

54 Stela at Silsila: see n. 52 above.

55 Porter and Moss 1972: 8; Kitchen 1968–90: IV, 83.

56 Porter and Moss 1972: 541; Kitchen 1968–90: IV, 83–84.

57 Porter and Moss 1960–64: 691, 695, 709, 712; Kitchen 1968–90: IV, 84–85.

58 pBM EA10683 [pChester Beatty III] (Kitchen 1968–90: IV, 85–88).

59 oCM CG25504 (Kitchen 1968–90: IV, 155).

60 See previous note.

61 pBologna 1086 (Kitchen 1968–90: 78–81).

62 The Bologna papyrus was written to a Memphite priest by his son.

63 oCM CG25504 (Kitchen 1968–90: IV, 155).

64 Kitchen 1968–90: III, 151–54, 467; IV: 100–01; Bohleke 1993: 356–68; Kahl 2007: 134–35. He was buried at Asyut.

65 TT23 (Porter and Moss 1960–64: 38–41; Kitchen 1968–90: II, 377; IV, 107–19; Kampp 1996: 206–09).

66 Kitchen 1968–90: IV, 120–22; Malek 1999: 601[801–643–110], 611–12 [801–643–370].

67 Kitchen 1968–90: IV, 102.

68 Kitchen 1968–90: IV, 103.

69 Kitchen 1968–90: IV, 103.

70 Kitchen 1968–90: IV, 102.

71 Kitchen 1968–90: IV, 104–06, 155; V, 257.

72 Rameses-emperre's father was a certain Yupa, a name borne by a man under Rameses II whose father had had a pure Hurrian name (Ruffle and Kitchen 1979: 71–74).

73 Kitchen 1968–90: IV, 124–25.

74 Kitchen 1968–90: IV, 123.

75 Kitchen 1968–90: IV, 125.

76 Kitchen 1968–90: III, 279–81; IV, 127.

77 Kitchen 1968–90: III, 207, 414–15; IV, 137, 292–93.

78 De Meuleneare 1968–72.

79 Vienna ÄS 5768 (Porter and Moss 1974–81: 838; Kitchen 1968–90: II, 883).

80 No contemporary monument attests to this, but it is stated in an autobiographical text of Roma-Roy himself (Cairo CG42186—Porter and Moss 1972: 146; Kitchen 1968–90: IV, 208–09).

81 Kitchen 1968–90: IV, 127–33, 208–10, 287–89; Bierbrier 1975: 4–5; Merenptah's seem to have been the cartouches erased in the earlier of Roma-Roy's Karnak tableaux (see fig. 69, below).

82 Kitchen 1968–90: III, 250; IV, 134.

83 Kitchen 1968–90: IV, 135.

84 Kitchen 1968–90: IV, 139–49.

85 Cf. Habachi 1980: 634 [21.–25.].

86 Porter and Moss 1952: 247; Habachi 1957: 33[34]; Kitchen 1968–90: IV: 94.

87 Porter and Moss 1952: 127 ; Kitchen 1968–90: IV, 96.

88 Porter and Moss 1952: 67 [1–2, 5], 68; Barguet et al. 1967: II, pl. c, ciii, civ; III, 1–2 [B 2, B 4], 57 [T 1, T 2]; V, pl. iv, viii[B 8a]; Kitchen 1968–90: IV, 1; Dodson 1997: 42–45.

89 Porter and Moss 1952: 80; Kitchen 1968–90: IV, 96.

90 Porter and Moss 1952: 25.

91 *Not* the tomb of the viceroy himself, as has been sometimes erroneously stated (Porter and Moss 1952: 80; Kitchen 1968–90: IV, 96).

92 Cairo JE40282 (Porter and Moss 1952: 73; Kitchen 1968–90: IV, 95; Caminos 1974: I, 17 n.17). Although generally attributed to Messuy, Caminos suggests that it could equally have belonged to the Khaemtjitry.

93 Emery and Kirwan 1935: 103–4.

94 Steindorff 1937: 198, pl. 44. Cf. Aubert and Aubert 1974: 124 and Krauss 1977: 134–35.

95 Cf. Mariette 1857: pl. 10, 13, 14.

96 Porter and Moss 1937: 256 [9B]; Kitchen 1968–90: IV, 96; Dodson 1997: 47.

97 Lepsius 1897–1913: IV, 175, could only read the terminal 𓏭 and restored *[Hw]y*; however, the reading *Msswy* has now been confirmed (Krauss 1997: 178–79).

98 The cartouche is now in a very poor condition (see Krauss 1997: 179).

99 Habachi was dubious that the two elements could be integral (1980: 639 n.117), with Murnane taking a similar view.

100 Porter and Moss 1952: 133[4W], 134[5W]; Kitchen 1968–90: IV, 97; it is possible that he could previously have been the Army Scribe of the name (p. 23, above).

101 Exc. no. 1745 (Kitchen 1968–90: IV, 282).

102 See H. S. Smith 1976: II, 150–151 nn. 1, 3; cf. Dodson 1997: 48, n. 54.

103 Kitchen 1968–90: IV, 159–60.

104 Porter and Moss 1960–64: 507–09; Thomas 1966: 108–111; Kitchen 1968–90: 68–72.

105 Dodson 2000a: 99–101.

106 Cf. Brock 1992.

107 Cairo JE87297 (Montet 1951: 111–18).

108 Cf. Ikram and Dodson 1998: 252–53.

109 Hayes 1935; Eaton-Krauss 1993.

110 Inc. BM EA49739 (Porter and Moss 1960–64: 509).

111 Cf. Reeves 1990a: 95.

112 pBM EA10185 [pSallier I] (Gauthier 1914: 421; Krauss 1976: 191–93).

113 oMMA 14.6.217; the month-number is missing, but the contents of oCM CG25509 make it clear that it must have been III (Kitchen 1968–90: IV, 298–299; cf. Hornung 2006: 212). On the long-disputed relationship between the death of Merenptah and the accession of Sethy II see next chapter.

114 Although the period of mummification was nominally seventy days, the actual interval between death and burial could vary considerably (cf. Ikram and Dodson 1998: 104, and Dodson 2009a: 88–90 for a case of possible delay for political reasons).

115 Reeves 1990a: 196–199, 232, 247. The mummy (Cairo CG61079—G. E. Smith 1912: 65–70) lacked its own coffin, being found in the trough of that of Sethnakhte (CG61039—Daressy 1909: 217–18).

116 Pasebkhanut's burial also included a usurped Eighteenth/Nineteenth Dynasty anthropoid stone coffin (Cairo JE85911—Montet 1951: 126–30), while Merenptah's Third Prophet of Amun, Amenhotep (see p. 24, above) had his coffin reused in the same tomb at Tanis for the General Wendjebaendjed (Tanis site museum—Montet 1951: 70–71).

117 A number of other royal tombs also lack their sarcophagus-coffers, or have had them smashed; for example, those of Amenhotep III, Sethy II, and Sethnakhte (cf. fig. 122, below).

118 Krogman and Baer 1980: 211.

119 Wente 1980: 260.

Chapter 2: After Merenptah

1 In at least one case (Cairo JE35126), one of the princely images has had a uraeus added (Sourouzian 1989: 117–18, pl. 22b).

2 Von Beckerath briefly espoused a third option that Amenmeses' was a rival of Siptah (1951: 70–76), but soon dropped it in favor of an alternate theory (1956: 246–47).

3 For the Thutmoside situation, and the long debate to which it gave rise, cf. Edgerton 1933.

4 Although Emery (1935–38: 356) did wonder whether the Sethy of KV14 (and bracelets JE52577–8: see fig. 76) might actually be a "Sethy III," the former viceroy of Kush of that name (Sethy Q—cf. above and pp. 85–86, below).

5 Formerly Liverpool M13510; (Porter and Moss 1972: 337 [called M13010]; [Mayer 1852: [13]; Gatty 1877: 48[303]; Emery 1935–38: 353–6; Petrie 1905: 119, 126, 127; Gauthier 1914: 129 n.1; von Beckerath 1951: 71; Helck 1955: 39; von Beckerath 1956: 244; Kitchen 1968–90: IV, 203; VII: 235; Dodson 1995: 125–28). Anecdote has it that the piece was found in the debris of the building after the war, but was accidentally consigned to the rubble used for the construction of the Otterspool Promenade along the Mersey.

6 Porter and Moss 1960–64: 532–33; Thomas 1966: 111–14.

7 For a full discussion of these, see Dodson 1999.

8 For which, see Brock 1992; on the possible fate of the outer sarcophagus intended for Sethy II, see Dodson 1986a, b; cf. Mojsov 1991/92. It should be noted that the head from the broken lid of the inner sarcophagus of Sethy II, now Louvre Museum (E 6205 Porter and Moss 1960: 533), is actually from the Nut-figure on its underside. The king's own head, together with most of the upper part of the lid, remains lost.

9 For those in Tutankhamun's KV62, see Reeves 1990b: 130–35; for fragments of similar figures from other royal tombs, cf. see Porter and Moss 1960: 553 (KV 34), 555 (KV 35), 560–1 (KV 43), 569 (KV 57).

10 Cf. Dodson 1999: 138–39 for some of the other explanations that have been put forward.

11 For the key discussions of these, see Krauss 1976; 1977: 159–67; Krauss 1997: 161–169; and Janssen 1997: 99–109.

12 Davies 1999: 33–34.

13 Janssen 1997: 100.

14 Cf. Janssen 1997: 99–109; Collier 2004: 2–8.

15 For an attempt to bolster this further by astronomical data see, Krauss 1997: 175–76; cf., however, Schneider 2010: 102–03.

16 Cf. Janssen 1997: 103–04.

17 Cf. Janssen 1997: 104; Collier 2004: 8.

18 Krauss 1976: 180–81; Krauss 1997: 165–69; cf. Janssen 1997: 100–102; Hornung 2006: 213.

19 Oracle-text (Porter and Moss 1952: 108–09; Kitchen 1968–90: IV, 275).

20 Porter and Moss 1952: 73; Kitchen 1968–90: IV, 274.

21 Porter and Moss 1937: 273; Kitchen 1968–90: IV, 273–74.

22 From Cemetery C, now UC16064 (Engelbach et al. 1915: pl. li[1]; Kitchen 1987; Dodson 1990a).

23 Cf. Kitchen 1996: 245–50.

24 The remains of a gate bearing figures of the king and his wife Tawosret have been found there (Pusch 1999); cf., however p. 160 n. 22, below.

25 Personal communication, Dylan Bickerstaffe.

26 Save some of the early speculations on the identity of the leading figure in the Medinet Habu processions of princes (see Kitchen 1972; 1982b).

27 In particular Krauss 1977: 131–45.

28 E.g. Habachi 1978: 66–67, as well as Yurco 1997 and others. As noted
   above, pp. 24–25, the existence of shabtis of Messuy is no evidence that he
   died as a viceroy, while his alleged tomb at Aniba is actually that of
   a colleague.
29 For full details of these, see Dodson 1997, with references.
30 Cf. Krauss 1977: 140–1, and further below.
31 As is done by Yurco 1997: 54.
32 See Dodson 1997: 45–46.
33 Horemheb: MMA 23.10.1 (Porter and Moss 1974–81: 865, from Memphis); Cairo
   CG42129 (Porter and Moss 1972: 107, from Karnak—headless); Paramesse:
   Cairo JE44863–4 (Porter and Moss 1972: 188, from Karnak); cf. Delvaux 1992.
34 Martin 1989: 70 72, pl. 68–71.
35 Prince Rameses C (Rameses IV) had a uraeus added in the "Games" scene
   in the forecourt of the Medinet Habu temple (Porter and Moss 1972: 493
   [67–69])— but not his brother, Amenhirkopeshef C (Rameses VI). It has now
   been recognized that the prince Sethhirkopeshef of tomb QV 43 was almost
   certainly the future Ramesses VIII (Hassanein 1985), but no royal insignia
   seem to have been added to his images there.
36 Cf. Kitchen 1972; 1982b.
37 Porter and Moss 1972: 51–52; Yurco 1979: 18–20[2].
38 Yurco 1979: 19–20.
39 Cairo CG1198 (Porter and Moss 1972: 52; Yurco 1979: 28–29).
40 Yurco 1979: 28 29 argued the original owner was Rameses II or Merenptah,
   but implicitly only because of his rejection of the possibility of Amenmeses
   ruling during Sethy's reign.
41 Cf. Dodson and Janssen 1989: 128–29.
42 oLouvre 666 (Kitchen 1968–90: II, 922–23; although undated, the list is
   written in the same handwriting as oLouvre 2261, which *is* dated.
43 On the possibility that Amenmeses may be mentioned in Year 53 of Rameses
   II, cf. Schneider 2011: 447–48
44 Cf. Dodson 1990b; there is one possible exception, with crown prince
   Amenemhat being appointed an Overseer of Cattle under Thutmose III.
45 Although Kozloff 2004 has suggested that the viceroy Amenhotep, attested
   late in the reign of Thutmose IV, might actually have been the crown prince
   Amenhotep D (the future Amenhotep III); this suggestion remains problematic
   and unlikely, given the certainly tender years of the prince at the time.
46 The last dated viceroy under Rameses II is Setau in Year 38 (Kitchen 1968–90:
   III, 104–07); most of the other viceroys attributable to the reign are very difficult
   to pin down in time (cf. Kitchen 1968–90: III, 68–113; Habachi 1980: 634).
47 Brand 2009; most were later recarved for Sethy II. On the lack of any
   replacement by the names of Amenmeses, see Brand 2009, *pace* Yurco 1986:
   197 and Kitchen 1968–90: IV, 194.
48 Brand 2009.
49 Porter and Moss 1972: 25–26; Kitchen 1968–90: IV, 257–59.
50 oCM CG25560 (Kitchen 1968–90: IV, 302).
51 oMMA 14.6.217 (Kitchen 1968–90: IV, 298).

52 oCM JE72452 (Gardiner 1954: 43 n.3; Thomas 1966: 115; Kitchen 1968–90: IV, 404; Valbelle 1985: 184–185; Helck 1990; Altenmüller 1992b: 148–150). There was in the past some debate as to whose Year 2 was involved, Gardiner proposing Siptah, but Helck and Altenmüller preferring Sethy II. The question has been settled by the discovery of a graffito of Siptah's Year 1 in the entrance of the tomb in question, KV14.

53 Although the Valley of the Queens tombs of Nefertiry (QV66) and her mother-in-law Tuya (QV80—Porter and Moss 1960–64: 769; Desroches-Noblecourt 1982: 232–35) were far more elaborate than the burial places of earlier New Kingdom royal wives: cf. Dodson 2003.

54 In spite of this, various writers have assumed that she had been a sister-wife of Sethy II; however, there is no evidence upon which to base such an assumption.

Chapter 3: The Reign of Amenmeses

1 H. S. Smith 1976: 130–1, 213–4 [1611]; pls. xxx[1], lxxvi[1]; Kitchen 1968–90: IV, 202[10.A]. The cartouche has been carved over an erased area (not mentioned in the publication, but clear in the photograph). The Horus name is original and not interfered with, and is certainly that of Amenmeses.

2 Cf. Hardwick 2006: 260.

3 Cf. Schaden and Ertman 1998: 154.

4 Porter and Moss 1960–64: 518; Ertman 1993: 39, 43–45; Schaden and Ertman 1998: 136–42; Schaden 2004: 135–36.

5 Schaden and Ertman 1998: 133–36.

6 Thomas 1966: 111; cf. Dodson 1987: 225. Lepsius had had doubts back in the 1840s, but had ultimately opted for linking Takhat and Baketwernel with Amenmeses (1897–1913: III, 206).

7 Schaden and Ertman 1998: 133–43.

8 The examples of members of the royal family shown in a king's tomb are restricted to the exceptional scene of Thutmose III with wives and daughters on a pillar in KV34 (Porter and Moss 1960–64: 553).

9 Brock 2003; Schaden 2004: 131.

10 Cf. those of Nefertiry D (Turin S.5153) and Meryetamun E (Berlin ÄM15274), for which see Habachi 1974.

11 She may have been the thirteenth daughter of Rameses II in the Luxor temple procession of princesses, where only the final -ḥb of her name is preserved.

12 Schaden 2004: 129–30.

13 Schaden 2004: 130.

14 Cf. the example of Iset D in QV51, who is always just "King's Mother" (of Rameses VI), even though she is known to have been a King's Great Wife of Rameses III (cf. Kitchen 1972: 189–192; 1982: 124).

15 Perhaps for members of the family of Rameses IX or X (Dodson 1987: 225–26; cf. Schaden and Ertman 1998: 149 n.149)?

16 Earl Ertman has suggested that the Baketwernel/Takhat decoration in any case should be dated to the Nineteenth Dynasty on iconographic grounds, based on parallels between the intrusion of parts of the KV10 figures into scene-borders, and similar instances seen in the KV14 and QV66 (Ertman 1993: 45; QV38 may

also be added to his list). However, the diagnostic feature in question is also to be seen in QV52 (Leblanc 1989: pl. cxxiv—ears of dog-headed deity), whose owner, Tyti, was a wife of Rameses III (Collier, Dodson and Hamernick 2010). Concerning the artistic style of the surviving queenly figure in KV 10, of Baketwernel, it is difficult to declare the image as anything more than simply Ramesside, albeit noting strong similarities with images of Queen Iset, mother of Ramesses VI, in QV 51 (e.g. Leblanc 1989: pl. cxi).

17 Cf. Schaden 2004: 130 n.4.
18 H. S. Smith 1976: 197, 214; Kitchen 1968–90: IV, 203.
19 Porter and Moss 1952: 118; Kitchen 1968–90: IV, 207.
20 Porter and Moss 1952: 161; Kitchen 1968–90: IV, 203; Spencer 1997: 40, 41, pl. 37d, 40c.
21 On a shrine at Tod (Kitchen 1968–90: IV, 202; later usurped by Rameses III) and on the pylon at Armant (Porter and Moss 1937: 157; Kitchen 1968–90: IV, 202); a jar bearing the king's name also came to light at Tell Edfu (Aksamit 2000).
22 Cf. below, p. 94, for potential posthumous memorials.
23 Porter and Moss 1972: 110; Yurco 1979: 25–26[6].
24 The head is now MMA 34.2.2 (Porter and Moss 1972: 52; Cardon 1979; Yurco 1979: 16–18[1]).
25 Porter and Moss 1972: 38; Yurco 1979: 21–25[4–5].
26 Now in the Hypostyle Hall (Porter and Moss 1972: 52; Yurco 1979: 20–21[3]).
27 BM EA26 (Porter and Moss 1972: 288; Kitchen 1968–90: IV, 267); Turin C.1383; Louvre A24 (Porter and Moss 1972: 291–92; Kitchen 1968–90: IV, 267–68).
28 Cairo TR 30/8/64/4 (Hardwick 2006).
29 Porter and Moss 1972: 112; Yurco 1979: 26.
30 The offering scene in Room III and Souls of Pe and Nekhen in Room XXXV (Porter and Moss 1972: 112, 123; Kitchen 1968–90: IV, 194–95).
31 Porter and Moss 1972: 211; Kitchen 1968–90: IV, 195.
32 See above.
33 Porter and Moss 1972: 81; Loeben 1987: 213, 217.
34 Porter and Moss 1960: 517–8; Thomas 1966: 110–11; Kitchen 1968–90: IV, 199–202; Ertman 1993; Schaden 1993, 1994, 2004; Schaden and Ertman 1998.
35 Porter and Moss 1972: 409; Kitchen 1968–90: IV, 195–97.
36 Cf. Maspero 1908: xvii–xviii; see also below p. 93.
37 Porter and Moss 1960–64: 683; Kitchen 1968–90: IV, 197; Krauss 1997: 180–81.
38 Porter and Moss 1972: 436; Kitchen 1968–90: IV, 197.
39 Porter and Moss 1972: 466–7; Kitchen 1968–90: IV, 197.
40 pBM EA10055 [pSalt 124] (Kitchen 1968–90: IV, 408–14).
41 $p3 ḥrwỉ$: Černý 1929: 252.
42 Surely not "a personal enemy of Neferhotep . . . perhaps Panēb" (Černý 1929: 247.
43 As first suggested by Černý (1929: 255–56); cf. Krauss 1977: 136–37.
44 Kitchen 1968–90: IV, 204–06.
45 Turin S.6037 (Kitchen 1968–90: IV, 205–06).
46 Vatican 156 (Porter and Moss 1960–64: 778; Kitchen 1968–90: IV, 205).

47 Cf. Habachi 1978: 64–65.
48 Porter and Moss 1952: 133; Kitchen 1968–90: IV, 97.
49 Turin S.6136 = N.50246 (Tosi and Roccati 1972: 202–3, 355) + Chicago OI 10816 (Kitchen 1968–90: IV, 206).
50 Porter and Moss 1960–64: 708; Dodson 1995.
51 Brooklyn L68.10.2.[48] (Fazzini 1972: 55–56); Chiddingstone Castle, Kent (ex-Rustafjaell Collection: Porter and Moss 1972: 377; Dodson 1995: 115–25); Liverpool M13827 (Kitchen 1968–90: IV, 203–04; Dodson 1995: 125–28).
52 Kitchen 1968–90: IV, 238.
53 Known from a number of sources dating to the reigns of Rameses II and Merenptah (Porter and Moss 1952: 79, 93; Kitchen 1968–90: III, 104, 118; IV, 98).
54 Porter and Moss 1952: 78–79, 118; Kitchen 1968–90: IV, 282–85; VII, 247. Kitchen dates them to Sethy II's reign, but none bears any king's name.
55 Porter and Moss 1972: 177; Kitchen 1968–60: IV, 210, 287–89.
56 Cf. Kitchen 1968–90: IV, 210.
57 Schaden and Ertman 1998: 120–125, 130–31, 135, 142.
58 Dodson 1992: 56–57.
59 Thomas 1966: 110.
60 Cf. Waddell 1940: 148–49 n.1.
61 Eusebius; Africanus has "Ammenephthês"; cf. Schneider 2011: 450-51.
62 As "Thuôris" conceals Tawosret: cf. p. 127, below.
63 Josephus, *Contra Apionem* I, 15, 16, §§98–102 (Waddell 1940: 102–05); cf. Schneider 2011.
64 Krauss 2000; 2001; cf. Görg 2000.

Chapter 4: Sethy II Restored

1 oCG25560; also found on Berlin ÄM12800, an obelisk from Athribis (Kitchen 1968–90: IV, 302; 244).
2 Except for the form of one particular sign: see p. 34, above.
3 Porter and Moss 1960–64: IV, 43; Kampp 1996: 212–13.
4 Kitchen 1968–90: IV, 271.
5 Analysed in Johnson and Brand 2013, replacing the conclusions reached in the original edition of the present work and in Dodson 2012: 13, 21-22.
6 Sa'ad 1975; cf. Dodson 2009a: 66–68. There is also the case of Mehy's appearance in Sethy I's battle reliefs (cf. p. 144 n. 25, above) and much later the late Twentieth Dynasty high priests of Amun, Amenhotep G and Herihor at Karnak (cf. Dodson 2012: 13, 21-22).
7 *imy-r sḏꜣwty ꜥ n tꜣ r ḏr.f.*
8 oCM CG25766 (Černý 1966; Kitchen 1968–90: IV, 286); though the name is damaged, Černý was confident that "Bay" was the most likely reading.
9 On the other hand, Posener 1977: 392–96 suggests that the ostracon might have been a satirical work against Bay, while Callender 2004: 91–92 would possibly date it to the last days of Bay's life, shortly before his execution.
10 Kitchen 1968–90: IV, 285–86.

11 Cf. Schulman 1986.
12 Combined in each case by prayers on his behalf by the king; cf. Blyth 1999: 42 who, however, fails to recognize that Bay was the original dedicatee, rather than Sethy-Merenptah B.
13 oCM CG25538, CG25515 (Kitchen 1968–90: IV, 315, 322).
14 Kitchen 1968–90: IV, 279–81.
15 pBM EA10055 [pSalt 124], rt. 1, 3 (Kitchen 1968–90: IV, 408).
16 Statue base Cairo CG1174 + BMA 37.1920E (Kitchen 1968–90: 258).
17 oCM JE72467 (Kitchen 1968–90: IV, 339).
18 Kitchen 1968–90: IV, 281, 357–62, 387–89; V, 376–78; VII, 247, 252.
19 Kitchen 1968–90: IV, 286–87, 339.
20 Kitchen 1968–90: IV, 287.
21 Cairo JE28705 (Kitchen 1968–90: IV, 294–95).
22 TT283 (Porter and Moss 1960–64: 365–66; Kampp 1996: 553–54).
23 Kitchen 1968–90: IV, 289–92.
24 Kitchen 1968–90: IV, 288.
25 Louvre A72 (Kitchen 1968–90: IV, 294); they may even have been brothers.
26 Kitchen 1968–90: IV, 296–97.
27 Cairo CG52577–8.
28 Porter and Moss 1960–64: 567; Thomas 1966: 155–56; for material recovered during reexcavation in 1999 see <http://www.nicholasreeves.com/item.aspx?category=Events&id=257>.
29 Aldred 1963b; Schneider 2003: 145–46.
30 Cf. Callender 2004: 93–94.
31 Cf. Gitton 1984; Schmidt 1994.
32 Schneider 2003: 141–46.
33 Porter and Moss 1972: 22; Kitchen 1968–90: IV, 250–51.
34 Kitchen 1968–90: IV, 264–66.
35 Kitchen 1968–90: IV, 262–63; cf. Brand 2009.
36 Kitchen 1968–90: IV, 269–71; Epigraphic Survey 1998: 6–7, pls. 143, 155–159, 172–173, 178, 194–195, 199–200, 204 and 224; cf. Brand 2009.
37 Kitchen 1968–90: IV, 271.
38 Cf. Blyth 1999: 40–42.
39 Cairo JE30283 (Pillet 1922: 253).
40 Cairo JE47296 (Pillet 1922: 252).
41 Quibell 1898: 9.
42 Hölscher 1951: pl. 36t—lower part only. Unprovenanced examples include Turin C.6388 (Fabretti, Rossi and Lanzone 1888: 248; Petrie 1925: 124, fig. 47); Cairo JE40426 (Pillet 1922: 253); Copenhagen Nationalmuseet Inv. 6640 (complete) and 11873 (lower part only), Leiden RMO G571 (Leemans 1841–82: II, pl. xliii); MMA 10.130.1677–81 (ex-Murch Collection, Hayes 1959: 362); and BM EA67970 (Parkinson 1999: 109 [31e]).
43 See Dodson 1999: 138.
44 Porter and Moss 1934: 167; Kitchen 1968–90: IV, 247–50.
45 Kitchen 1968–90: IV, 242–43.
46 Kitchen 1968–90: IV, 243–44; Pusch 1999.

47 Kitchen 1968–90: IV, 245–46.
48 Kitchen 1968–90: IV, 246; El-Sawi 1990; cf. Cabrol 1993.
49 Kitchen 1968–90: IV, 247.
50 Kitchen 1968–90: IV, 250.
51 oCG25515 (Kitchen 1968–90: IV, 382).
52 Hornung 2006: 213.
53 Rather than the astronomical ceiling used since the time of Sethy I, a crude figure of Nut was painted on the ceiling. On the left wall are two registers of divinities, with three mummiform figures below; on the right are two registers of divinities in shrines, with an enshrined Anubis-jackal nearest the entrance doorway.
54 MMA 10.130.1074 A–B (Gift of Helen Miller Gould, 1910, from the collection of Chauncey Murch), mentioned in Hayes 1959: 362. Both pieces, comprising the lower portion of the legs and feet, bear only the nomen "Sethy-Merenptah," and there seems to be nothing to distinguish them from the numerous smaller faience examples of Sethy I. My thanks go to Diane Craig Patch for access to these objects.
55 Altenmüller 1984; 1985: 14; 1992b: 148, Abb. 19.
56 Altenmüller 1992b: 159–60.
57 pBM EA10055 [pSalt 124], recto 1, 11–12 [Kitchen 1968–90: IV, 409]).
58 Paneb was certainly still in office in Siptah's Year 2, but proposals for the ending of his career have had him variously executed in Siptah's Year 6, or even continuing in office down to the beginning of the Twentieth Dynasty (see Davies 1999: 36).
59 Kitchen 1968–90: VI, 146.
60 Active during that reign and last attested in Year 1 of Rameses V (Peden 1994a: 60); Reeves (1990a: 234, 247–48) attributes the Year 6 instead to the late-Twentieth Dynasty *whm-mswt*.
61 Cairo CG61036 (Porter and Moss 1960–64: 555).
62 Cairo CG61040 (ibid).
63 Cairo CG61074 (G. E. Smith 1912: 46–51; Piacentini and Orsenigo 2004: 178–79, 204–05).
64 Piacentini and Orsenigo 2004: 178–79, 208–09.
65 Cairo CG61081 (G. E. Smith 1912: 73–81).
66 Wente and Harris 1992: 10–11; the mummy-docket was unpublished at the time their paper was written.
67 Krogman and Baer 1980: 206–07.
68 Although if Sethy were not the father of Amenmeses, and were a late-born (even if eldest surviving) son of Merenptah, he could have died in his twenties (cf. Wente 1980: 262–63).
69 Cf. Robins 1981.
70 Reeve and Adams 1993.
71 Molleson and Cox 1993: 169.
72 The latter case neatly matches the case of the "50:0–55:0+" year old Rameses II; cf. Bickerstaffe 2009: 69–70.
73 G. E. Smith 1912: 73.
74 Cf. Bickerstaffe 2009: 101.

Chapter 5: Siptah

1 See above, p. 79, for his probable actual date of death and Siptah's accession.
2 oCM CG25515 (Kitchen 1968–90: IV, 382).
3 Porter and Moss 1952: 98, 99; Kitchen 1968–90: IV, 362–63.
4 Kitchen 1968–90: IV, 345.
5 Porter and Moss 1952: 134; Kitchen 1968–90: IV, 374.
6 Louvre N442A, N5418 (Porter and Moss 1974–81: 785; Kitchen 1968–90: IV, 344; a third "canopic" jar listed by Kitchen is dittography of N442A: (Catherine Bridonneau, personal communication 3 June 2009).
7 Louvre N442B (Porter and Moss 1974–81: 785; Kitchen 1968–90: VI, 451).
8 Cf. Gardiner 1954.
9 Cf. Gardiner's recantation, 1958.
10 For this name see p. 93, below.
11 Porter and Moss 1937: 245; Kitchen 1968–90: IV: 363–64.
12 Porter and Moss 1937: 211.
13 Breasted 1906–07: 274, 275, 278, 279; cf. Maspero 1908: xix.
14 Cf. Gardiner 1958: 17–18.
15 Porter and Moss 1972: 386; Kitchen 1968–90: IV, 370.
16 Piacentini and Orsenigo 2004: 180–81, 208–09.
17 CG61080: G. E. Smith 1912: 70–73.
18 Krogman and Baer 1980: 206–07.
19 Molleson and Cox 1993: 167–79.
20 The Festival of Min reliefs in the memorial temple of Rameses III at Medinet Habu (Porter and Moss 1972: 500). This attenuated "official" list may have contributed to the confusion seen in the Nineteenth Dynasty sections of Manetho (cf. p. 67, above, and p. 127, below).
21 Cf. Dodson 2009a: 71, 132–5.
22 pBM EA9999 [pHarris I = Great Harris Papyrus], §75,4–5 (Grandet 2005: pl. 76).
23 Although a very different interpretation was put forward by Goedicke (1979), who read the passage as referring to Egypt's Asiatic dependencies, rather than Egypt itself. However, this seems to be against the Egyptocentric context of the papyrus as a whole, and the clear indication in Sethnakhte's Elephantine stela (see below, pp. 119–20) that he had to fight for the rule of Egypt—not simply to reassert Egyptian authority in Syria-Palestine (in spite of Goedicke's further attempt (1996) to read the text of this monument in a contrary manner).
24 Goedicke argued that the name was actually "Su" (the *i.ir* being a form of the verb *iri* [1976: 6–7]) who might be none other than Saul of the Old Testament.
25 In the legal text in the Saqqara tomb of Mose (Gaballa 1977: 25).
26 Cf. S. Redford 2002: 75–76. In this case the man's real name may have been Meryre—"The one loved by Re."
27 Helck 1955: 42; 1971: 232–33; von Beckerath 1956: 249.
28 Schneider 2003: 139 (*eine andere Zeit war entstanden nach dieser mit leeren Jahren als "Der, dersechs Jahre regierte", ein Syrer, Fürst war unter ihnen* [I owe the English translation used here to the kindness of Jürgen Schesser]).

29 Schneider derives this meaning by replacing the ⌐-determinative of the "name" Irsu with ⸗, and taking the ⸗ of "Irsu" as a phonetic writing of the numeral "6" (Schneider 2003: 138–140).

30 See below.

31 For this equation see Vandier 1971; for strong doubts and a listing of the monuments of the prince(s) Rameses-Siptah, see Fisher 2001: I, 118–19; II, 181–82.

32 Schneider 2003: 140–41.

33 The daughter of Hattusilish III.

34 Cf. von Beckerath 1951: 77, 1962: 71, 74.

35 Fisher 2001: I, 118–19; II, 181–82.

36 Aldred 1963a.

37 Such subterranean collisions were not particularly uncommon in the Valley of the Kings; for another example, see below p. 124.

38 Jenni (ed.) in preparation; <http://pages.unibas.ch/talderkoenige/aktuell.htm>.

39 Most recently by Hardwick 2006: 260 n.18.

40 Gl.122 (Malek 1999: 70–71).

41 von Beckerath 1962, seconded by (for exmample) Callender 2004: 88; 2006: 52 and Hardwick 2006: 260 n.18.

42 Lesko 1966: 31.

43 Drenkhahn 1980: 35–8, 53.

44 Aldred 1963a: 45–46.

45 A small bronze naos allegedly once in the British Museum (Prisse d'Avennes 1847: 715); John Taylor tells me that this piece cannot be identified in the collection today.

46 Reading "Akhre," rather than the correct "Akhenre," and of course uncollatable in view of the disappearance of the object.

47 Cairo JE8774 (Porter and Moss 1937: 51; Kitchen 1968–90: II, 550; Krauß 1977: 157).

48 Cf. above, p. 47.

49 Cf. Kitchen 1993ff(b): 380.

50 See (e.g.) Dorman 1988: 18–43.

51 Cairo JE43341 (Porter and Moss 1934: 40; Kitchen 1968–90: IV, 341–43).

52 Cf. her appearance in a number of reliefs at Karnak (Gabolde 2005).

53 Porter and Moss 1960–64: 527–32; Thomas 1966: 114–15, 125; Altenmüller 1983a–b; 1985; 2001; 2012. McCarthy 2008.

54 Cf. the remarks of Gardiner (1958: 18) and Callender (2004: 88–89) on the potential significance of the placement of Siptah's images in the tomb as a means of emphasizing his dependence on Tawosret.

55 Kitchen 1968–90: IV, 366.

56 Porter and Moss 1952: 69; Kitchen 1968–90: IV, 366.

57 Cf. Romer 1974.

58 Porter and Moss 1960–64: 527; Thomas 1966: 115–16; Kitchen 1968–90: IV, 355–56; Altenmüller 1989; 1992a; 1994a.

59 Cairo JE72451 (Kitchen 1968–90: IV, 404).

60 Cf. Ryan 1992; all other non-royal tombs in the Valley are simple shaft- or corridor-tombs.

61 See Dodson and Ikram 2008: 265–66.

62 On the basis that a fragmentary text in the tomb naming Queen Nubkhesbed, wife of Rameses VI (Altenmüller 1994c: 5–6 who, however, associates it with another burial in the tomb—see n. 64 below).

63 Altenmüller 1994a: 4–5.

64 Altenmüller 1994c.

65 Cairo JE25764 (Porter and Moss 1934: 59; Kitchen 1968–90: IV, 369.

66 One still in situ, one MFA 88.747 (Porter and Moss 1934: 8; Kitchen 1968–90: IV, 369; V, 3; Spencer (ed.) 2007: 58–59).

67 Porter and Moss 1934: 8; Kitchen 1968–90: IV, 369.

68 Cf. Callender 2004: 89–90.

69 The exact date is unclear, but was some time before the end of the Late Helladic IIIB ceramic phase (c. early twelfth century BC).

70 Freu 1988.

71 Copenhagen Ny Carlsberg ÆIN134 (Jørgensen 1998: 118–19[39]).

72 Dodson 2004: 81.

73 Graffiti of the Viceroy Sethy at Sehel and of the soon-to-be-Viceroy Hori (II) at Buhen (Porter and Moss 1937: 251; 1952: 134; Kitchen 1968–90: IV, 363, 364); for the latter, see fig. 99.

74 See previous note.

75 Porter and Moss 1952: 134; Kitchen 1968–90: IV, 135; he was a former "Royal Envoy" previously active in Nubia: see n. 73 above.

76 Cf. Caminos 1974: I, 92–95.

77 Kitchen 1968–90: IV, 357–61.

78 Porter and Moss 1937: 211; Kitchen 1968–90: IV, 373.

79 Östergötlands Länsmuseum, Linköping, 189 (Malek 1999: 611; Kitchen 1968–90: IV, 375.

80 Kitchen 1968–90: IV, 377–78.

81 Kitchen 1968–90: IV, 345; Lauffray, Sa'ad, and Sauneron 1975: 28, pl. ix.

82 Kitchen 1968–90: IV, 353.

83 Vatican 22670 (Malek 199: 71).

84 Porter and Moss 1972: 429 (Kitchen 1968–90: 346–47).

85 Ashmolean E.3392; Berlin ÄM13363; Cairo JE31417–8; Chicago OI 1360–61; Petrie UC14375–6, 15984–7; Copenhagen Nationalmuseet 6650–72; Manchester Museum 2751–2; Marseilles 236; UPMAA E.2136–7.

86 These derive from an estate of "Sethy-Merenptah in the House of Amun" (Petrie 1897: 29). It is unclear whether this was an establishment connected with the late Sethy II or a much older foundation of the first King Sethy.

87 Petrie 1897: 15.

88 Porter and Moss 1960–64: 564–66; Jenni (ed.) in preparation.

89 Cf. Dodson 1994: 72–73, 127.

90 oIFAO 1864 = oDM 886 (Grandet 2000; 2003: 59–60, 291–92).

Chapter 6: The Reign of Tawosret

1 oCairo CG25293 (Kitchen 1968–90: IV, 414; Altenmüller 1996, replacing his earlier view that this might be a burial of Bay in Year 4 [1992b: 163 n.31]).

2 Cf. Hornung 2006: 213; as noted below, Siptah's successor continued his regnal year-count.

3   Cf. e.g. the 273/274 day gap between the death of Meresankh III and her burial (Dunham and Simpson 1974: 8) and the apparent six-month-long gap between Tutankhamun's death and burial (Bryce 1990: 104–05).

4   It has been suggested that this may have been a precursor to an intended joint burial of Tawosret and Sethy II in the tomb (Altenmüller 1983: 40–43; cf. Callender 2004: 96–97); however, this seems unlikely, especially as Sethy had by then been dead for over half a decade.

5   Cf. the treatment of Smenkhkare by the post-Amarna kings (Dodson 2009a: 138).

6   Cf. Callender 2004: 94–95.

7   In one place in KV14 only (Gardiner 1954: 42–43, from Lepsius 1849–1859: III, pl. 206b; 1897–1913: III, 213). Porter and Moss 1964: 530, following the opinions of Lepsius, Brugsch, and Bouriant, suggests that the lady might rather be associated with Sethnakhte's usurpation of the tomb.

8   Cf. Altenmüller 1992b: 147–54, 159.

9   Altenmüller 1992b: 153–54, 156–57, fig. 24–25.

10 Perhaps around the II ꜣḥt 18 in Year 6 that is included in a graffito in this part of the tomb, which must have fallen close to Siptah's death and thus Tawosret's change of status (cf. Altenmüller 1992b: 153–54). This abortive new hall is represented vestigially by two small chambers on either side of the axis, just beyond the first hall (Ka/b).

11 Until Altenmüller's research in the tomb, this extension was often attributed to the usurpation of KV14 for Sethnakhte: cf. p. 126, below.

12 Altenmüller 1994: 4–5; Callender 2004: 99–101.

13 Although Altenmüller 1983: 140–43 would prefer to see it as a sarcophagus to be used for Sethy II's putative interment in the tomb (cf. n.4, above).

14 Porter and Moss 1972: 447; Wilkinson (ed.) 2011; Wilkinson 2012; Creasman, Johnson, McClain and Wilkinson 2014.

15 Cairo CG16063–121; JE31415; Petrie UC12839, 12843 14377, 29391–2, 29436–7; MMA 21.2.89–108; UPMAA E.2126.

16 Apart from possibly some wine-jar dockets mentioning an estate of a "Sethy-Merenptah," also mentioned on the dockets from Siptah's temple (cf. p. 159 n.86, above).

17 Wilkinson 2011; 2012.

18 Wilkinson 2011; 2012

19 Perhaps after completion by Sethnakhte?

20 Cairo, Grand Egyptian Museum (Bakry 1971b; Kitchen 1968-90: IV, 352; Drenkhahn 1981; Bassir 2013).

21 MMA 28.9.8 and 32.2.44 (Kitchen 1968–90: IV, 352).

22 Pusch 1999; this apparently depicted Tawosret standing behind Sethy II, although whether as queen-consort or queen-regnant is not altogether clear (Callender 2004: 97–98).

23 Cairo JE45568 (Kitchen 1968–90: IV, 353).

24 Kitchen 1968–90: IV, 353.

25 Lesko 1966: 29, pl. xiii.

26 Kitchen 1968–90: IV, 351.

27 Kitchen 1968–90: IV, 351.
28 MacGillivray 2006; it is possible that Sethnakhte may have taken over Ta-wosret's Theban now-destroyed memorial temple.
29 Kitchen 1968–90: IV, 356.
30 As queen: Cairo CG53260; as king: MMA 07.228.212 (Kitchen 1968–90: IV, 373).
31 Most now in Cairo, the rest in Berlin and the MMA (Porter and Moss 1934: 34–35; Hayes 1959: 358–60).
32 Louvre A71=N72 (Porter and Moss 1974–81: 865–66; Kitchen 1968–90: IV, 379–81).
33 Kitchen 1968–90: IV, 376–77.
34 oIFAO DM 594; oCairo CG25293 (Kitchen 1968–90: IV, 407–08).

Chapter 7: Downfall, Renaissance, and Decline

1 Especially given his name's incorporation of that of Seth, common in the family since before the accession of Rameses I.
2 Kitchen 1968–90: V, 671–672; Goedicke 1996.
3 On these Asiatics, cf. Kahn 2010.
4 pBM EA9999, §75,4–5 (Grandet 2005: pl. 76).
5 Parkinson 1997: 131–43; Quirke 2004: 135–39.
6 Cf. Dodson 2009a: 63–5, 117–9.
7 The most plausible previous alternative, that the restorations were carried out by Bay during a putative period of rule that witnessed a civil war between Tawosret and Sethnakhte, ceased to be an option as soon as his execution in Year 5 became known.
8 Cf. Bierbrier 2001: 585.
9 The existence of such was accepted by many earlier scholars (for example, Breasted 1905: 473–4, although in this case placed at the end of an AmenmesesSiptah-Sethy II succession).
10 In some cases with both epithets together.
11 oPetrie UC19614 (Kitchen 1968–90: V, 1–2).
12 Boriak 2008/9.
13 Cairo CG42159 (Porter and Moss 1972: 146; Kitchen 1968–90: V, 7).
14 Cairo CG581, CG42160 (Porter and Moss 1972: 146, 262; Kitchen 1968–90: V, 397–98); other material bears no royal name (Kitchen 1968–90: V, 398–99).
15 oIFAO DM 148 (Kitchen 1968–90: V, 505).
16 Cf. Hornung 2006: 214 on the apparent ten-year gap between Year 7 of Tawosret and Year 7 of Rameses III.
17 von Beckerath 1994: 77, n.431.
18 Stockholm Medelhavsmuseet E.1393 (Porter and Moss 1952: 161; Kitchen 1968–90: V, 2).
19 Porter and Moss 1952: 350; Kitchen 1968–90: V, 1.
20 Porter and Moss 1934: 8, 30, 62; 1974–81: 832, 861; 1972: 256; Kitchen 1968–90: V, 4.
21 Porter and Moss 1960–64: 707–708; Kitchen 1968–90: V, 3–4.
22 Porter and Moss 1960–64: 518–27; Thomas 1966: 125–27.
23 Cf. how much of Sethy II's tomb seems to have been cut and its decoration laid out before Amenmeses' seizure of power (see pp. 32–33, above). The old view

that the tomb was abandoned by Sethnakhte directly following the collision is therefore unlikely.

24 Suggestions that her mummy may have found its way to KV35 are unlikely: cf. n. 30 below.

25 pTurin C.1879 (Kitchen 1968–90: V, 337; f. Callender 2004: 87).

26 Perhaps through conflation with Siptah—not surprisingly in view of Tawosret's continuation of her late ward's regnal years.

27 Africanus; a similar note exists in the Armenian version of Eusebius (Waddell 1940: 148–49, 152–53).

28 Cairo JE20395, JE36331, Brussels E584 (Porter and Moss 1937: 43, 51; Kitchen 1968–90: V, 5–6).

29 Cairo CG61039, CG61044 (Porter and Moss 1960–64: 555). The inner coffin is made simply of cartonnage, contrasting with the solid gold of Tutankhamun's corresponding piece, and the single log of cedar from which that of Rameses III was crafted. This suggests a degree of poverty in Sethnakhte's internment.

30 Cairo CG61082 (G. E. Smith 1912: 81–84); this has frequently been posited as being the body of Tawosret, but there is no evidence for this, other than her previous ownership of Sethnakhte's tomb. Indeed, it is highly unlikely that she would have been allowed to share her victor's burial place. It has also been suggested that Sethnakhte might have been the "mummy on the boat" in KV35 (cf. Bickerstaffe 2009: 102), but there is likewise no evidence for this and the position of the arms (along the sides, rather than crossed at the breast, as *de rigeur* for kings since the time of Amenhotep I) is definitive against the proposition. Most likely is that Sethnakhte's mummy was destroyed by robbers and his empty coffin was used as a convenient container by the Twenty-first Dynasty reburial commissioners.

31 For a general account of the reign, see Grandet 1993.

32 O'Connor 2000.

33 For this and an overview of Egypto-Libyan relations in the Ramesside Period, see Kitchen 1990.

34 Cf. Kitchen 1982b and Bierbrier 2001.

35 Cf. Frandsen 1991.

36 For one recent reconstruction of the events see S. Redford 2002, although there remains much debate on various aspects of the so-called "Harem Conspiracy"; on the queens of Rameses III, cf. Collier, Dodson and Hamernik 2010.

37 For whom, see Peden 1994a.

38 On the order of succession, cf. Kitchen 1972, 1982b, 1984. The backgrounds to these "irregular" successions are unknown, in spite of (for example) Černý's confident assersion of conflict between Rameses V and VI (1965: 8–11).

39 Peet 1930.

40 Wente 1966; Morales 2001; Dodson 2012:13-16.

41 This has been seen as a revolt by the viceroy of Nubia, but the situation may have been more complex: cf. Thijs 2003 and Dodson 2012: 18-21.

42 pMoscow 120 (Gardiner 1932: 60-76; Korostovtsev 1960). The question of whether the document is a genuine report, a literary work based on fact, or even a

work of ficition has been much debated (cf. for example, Goedicke 1975; Egberts 1998); Jaroslav Černý took the view that the way in which the text had been written on the papyrus indicates that it is indeed an original report (1952: 22).

43 Thijs 1998; 1999a–b; 2000a–b; 2001a–b; 2003; 2004a–b; the rebuttals of von Beckerath (2000: 114–16, 2001: 17) by no means negate Thijs' arguments. Under his thesis, Rameses XI was recognized nationally during only the last decade of his ~30-year reign: perhaps significant here is that his prenomen used the epithet "setepenptah"—the only royal prenomen regularly to invoke Ptah, the patron god of Memphis. All other pre-Ptolemaic prenomina to invoke the god were apparently "specials," for use at Memphis only (for example, Daressy 1900: 143 [Shoshenq I]), suggesting that at his advent, Rameses XI could indeed have been a northern monarch. See further Dodson 2012: 9-13.

BIBLIOGRAPHY

Abbreviations used for periodicals

AncEg   *Ancient Egypt* (Manchester: Ancient Egypt Magazine).

ASAE   *Annales du Service des Antiquités de l'Égypte* (Cairo: Institut français d'Archéologie orientale; Supreme Council of Antiquities Press).

BAR   *Biblical Archaeology Review* (Washington: Society for Biblical Archaeology).

BES   *Bulletin of the Egyptological Seminar* (New York: Egyptological Seminar of New York).

BIFAO   *Bulletin de l'Institut français d'Archéologie orientale du Caire* (Cairo: Institut français d'Archéologie orientale).

BiOr   *Bibliotheca Orientalis* (Leiden: Nederlands Instituut voor het Nabije Oosten).

BSEG   *Bulletin de la Societé d'Égyptologie de Genève* (Geneva: Bulletin de la Societé d'Égyptologie de Genève).

BSFE   *Bulletin de la Societé française d'Égyptologie* (Paris: Societé française d'égyptologie).

CdE   *Chronique d'Égypte* (Brussels: Fondation égyptologique Reine Elisabeth).

CRAIBL   *Comptes rendus des séances de l'Academie des inscriptions et belles letters* (Paris: l'Academie des inscriptions et belles letters).

DE   *Discussions in Egyptology* (Oxford: DE Publications).

165

EgArch   *Egyptian Archaeology: Bulletin of the Egypt Exploration Society* (London: Egypt Exploration Society).

GM   *Göttinger Miszellen* (Gšttingen: Universität Göttingen. Ägyptologisches Seminar).

IEJ   *Israel Exploration Journal* (Jerusalem: Israel Exploration Society).

JARCE   *Journal of the American Research Center in Egypt* (New York, &c: Eisenbraun).

JEA   *Journal of Egyptian Archaeology* (London: Egypt Exploration Fund/Society).

JEH   *Journal of Egyptian History* (Leiden: Brill)

JNES   *Journal of Near Eastern Studies* (Chicago: University of Chicago Press).

JSSEA   *Journal of the Society for the Study of Egyptian Antiquities* (Toronto: Society for the Study of Egyptian Antiquities).

Kmt   *Kmt: a Modern Journal of Ancient Egypt* (San Francisco: Kmt Communications).

LÄ   *Lexikon der Ägyptologie* (Wiesbaden: Otto Harrassowitz, 1975–).

MDAIK   *Mitteilungen des Deutschen Archäologischen Instituts, Kairo* (Mainz: Philipp von Zabern).

MMJ   *Metropolitan Museum Journal.* (New York: Metropolitan Museum of Art).

NARCE   *Newsletter of the American Research Center in Egypt* (Various locations: American Research Center in Egypt).

OMRO   *Oudheidkundige Mededelingen uit het Rijksmuseum van Oudheden te Leiden* (Leiden: Rijksmuseum van Oudheden).

PSBA   *Proceedings of the Society of Biblical Archaeology* (London: Society of Biblical Archaeology).

RdE   *Revue d'Egyptologie* (Leuven: Peeters).

RT   *Recueil de Travaux relatifs à la Philologie et à l'Archéologie égyptiennes et assyriennes* (Paris: A. Franck).

SAK   *Studien zur altägyptschen Kultur* (Hamburg: H. Buske Verlag).

TSBA   *Transactions of the Society for Biblical Archaeology* (London: Longmans, Green, Reader and Dyer).

WZKM   *Wiener Zeitschrift für Kunde des Morgenlandes* (Vienna: Wiener Universität—Institute für Orientalistik).

ZÄS   *Zeitschrift für Ägyptische Sprache und Altertumskunde* (Leipzig: J. C. Hinrichs'sche Buchhandlung/Berlin: Akademie Verlag).

ZDMG   *Zeitschrift der Deutschen Morgenländischen Gesellschaft* (Wiesbaden: Kommissionsverlag F. Steiner).

List of works cited

Aksamit, J. 2000. "Egyptian Faience Jar with a Cartouche of Amenmesse from Tell Edfu—the New Kingdom in the Polish-French Excavations in 1937." In *Civilisations du Bassin méditerranéen: hommages à Joachim Śliwa*, edited by K. M. Ciałowicz and J. A. Ostrowski, 29–33. Krakow: Université Jagaellonne, Institut d'Archéologie.

Aldred, C. 1963a. "The Parentage of King Siptah." *JEA* 49: 41–48.

——— 1963b. "Valley Tomb no. 56 at Thebes." *JEA* 49: 176–78.

——— 1968. "Two Monuments of the Reign of Ḥoremḥeb." *JEA* 54: 100–106.

——— 1978. *Jewels of the Pharaohs*. London and New York: Thames and Hudson.

Altenmüller, H. 1982. "Tausret und Sethnacht." *JEA* 68: 107–15.

——— 1983a. "Das Grab des Königin Tausret im Tal des Könige von Thebes: Erster Vorbericht über die Arbeiten des Archäologischen Instituts der Universität Hamburg im Winter 1982/1983." *SAK* 10: 1–24.

——— 1983b. "Rolle und Bedeutung des Grabes der Königin Tausret im Königsgrabertal von Theben." *BSEG* 8: 3–11.

——— 1984. "Der Begräbungstag Sethos' II." *SAK* 11: 37–47.

——— 1985. "Das Grab der Königin Tausret (KV 14). Bericht über eine archäologische Unternehmung." *GM* 84: 7–17.

——— 1989. "Untersuchungen zum Grab des Bai (KV 13) im Tal der Könige von Theben." *GM* 107: 43–54.

——— 1992a. "Zweiter Vorbericht in die Arbeiten des Archäologischen Instituts der Universität Hamburg am Grab des Bay (KV 13) im Tal der Könige von Theben." *SAK* 19: 15–36.

——— 1992b. "Bemerkungen zu den neu gefundenen Daten im Grab der Königin Twosre (KV 14) im Tal der Könige von Theben." In *After Tut'ankhamūn*, edited by C. N. Reeves, 141–164. London and New York: Kegan Paul International.

——— 1994a. "Dritter Vorbericht in die Arbeiten des Archäologischen Instituts der Universität Hamburg am Grab des Bay (KV 13) im Tal der Könige von Theben." *SAK* 21: 1–18.

——— 1994b. "Das Graffito 551 aus der thebanischen Nekropole." *SAK* 21: 19–28.

——— 1994c. "Prinz Mentu-her-chopeschef aus der 20. Dynastie." *MDAIK* 50: 1–12.

—— 1995. "Die verspätete Beisetzung des Siptah." *GM* 145: 29–36.

—— 1996. "Das präsumtive Begräbnis des Siptah." *SAK* 23: 1–9.

—— 1999. "Zwei Ostraka und ein Baubefund. Zum Tod des Schatzkanzlers Bay im 3. Regierungsjahr des Siptah." *GM* 171: 13–18.

—— 2001. "The Tomb of Tausert and Setnakht." In *The Treasures of the Valley of the Kings*, edited by K. R. Weeks, 222–231. Cairo: The American University in Cairo Press.

Aston, D. A. and E. B. Pusch. 1999. "The Pottery from the Royal Horse Stud and its Stratigraphy. The Pelizaeus Museum Excavation at Qantir/Per-Ramesses, Sector Q IV." *Ägypten und Levante* 9: 39–75.

Aubert, J.-F. and L. Aubert. 1974. *Statuettes égyptiennes, Chaouabtis, ouchebtis.* Paris: Librairie d'Amérique et d'Orient Adrien Maisonneuve.

Bakry, H. S. K. 1971a. "Recent Discoveries in the Delta." *Revista delgi Studi Orientali* 46: 1–15.

—— 1971b. "The Discovery of a Statue of Queen Twosre (1202–1194? B.C.) at Madinet Nasr, Cairo." *Revista delgi Studi Orientali* 46: 17–26.

Barguet, P. 1952. "Tôd. Rapport de fouilles de la saison février-avril 1950." *BIFAO* 51: 50–110.

—— 1962. *Le temple d'Amon-Rê à Karnak.* Cairo: Institut français d'Archéologie orientale.

Barguet, P. et al. 1967. *Le temple d'Amada*, 5 vols. Cairo: Centre de Documentation et d'Études sur l'ancienne Égypte.

Bickel, S. 1997. *Untersuchungen im Totentempel des Merenptah in Theben, III: Tore und andere wiederverwendete Bauteile Amenophis' III.* Stuttgart: Franz Steiner Verlag.

Bickerstaffe, D. 2009. *Refugees for Eternity: the Royal Mummies of Thebes. Part Four: Identifying the Royal Mummies.* UK: Canopus Press.

Bierbrier, M. L. 1975. *The Late New Kingdom in Egypt (c. 1300–664 B.C.).* Warminster: Aris and Phillips.

—— 2001. "What's in a Name?" *Archiv orientální* 69: 583–85.

—— (forthcoming). "Bye-bye Bay." In *Ramesside Studies in Honour of K. A. Kitchen*, edited by M. Collier and S. Snape. Bolton: Rutherford Press.

Blyth, E. 1999. "Some Thoughts on Seti II: 'the good-looking young pharaoh.'" In *Studies on Ancient Egypt in Honour of H. S. Smith*, edited by A. Leahy and W. J. Tait, 39–42. London: Egypt Exploration Society.

Bohleke, B. 1993. *The Overseers of Double Granaries of Upper and Lower Egypt in the Egyptian New Kingdom, 1570–1085 B.C.* New Haven: Yale University Press.

Boriak, M. 2008/9. "Re-writing Egypt's history: the Stela of Bakenkhonsu." *AncEg* 9/3: 24–27.

Bordreuil, P. 1987. "Decouvertes épigraphiques récentes à Ras Ibn Hani et à Ras Shamra." *CRAIBL* 1987: 289–301.

Botti, G. and P. Romanelli. 1951. *Le sculture del Museo Gregoriano Egizio.* Vatican City: Tip. poliglotta vaticana.

Brand, P. J. 2000. *The Monuments of Seti I: Epigraphic, Historical and Art Historical Analysis.* Leiden: Brill.

——— 2009. "Usurped Cartouches of Merenptah at Karnak and Luxor." In *Causing His Name to Live: Studies in Egyptian History and Epigraphy in Memory of William J. Murnane,* edited by P. Brand and L. Cooper, 29–48. Leiden: Brill Academic Publishers.

——— 2011. "The date of war scenes on the south wall of the Great Hypostyle Hall and the west wall of the Cour de la Cachette at Karnak and the history of the late Nineteenth Dynasty." In *Ramesside Studies in Honour of K. A. Kitchen,* edited by M. Collier and S. Snape, 51–84 Bolton: Rutherford Press.

Breasted, J. H. 1905. *A history of Egypt: from the earliest times to the Persian conquest.* New York: Scribner.

——— 1906–07. *Ancient records of Egypt, historical documents from the earliest times to the Persian conquest,* 5 vols. Chicago: University of Chicago Press.

Brock, E. C. 1992. "The Tomb of Merenptah and its Sarcophagi." In *After Tut'ankhamūn,* edited by C. N. Reeves, 122–140. London and New York: Kegan Paul International.

——— 2003. "The Sarcophagus Lid of Queen Takhat." In *Egyptology at the Dawn of the Twenty-First Century: Proceedings of the Eighth International Congress of Egyptologists, Cairo, 2000,* 1, edited by Z. Hawass and L. P. Brock, 97–102. Cairo: The American University in Cairo Press.

Bruyère, B. 1930. *Mert Seger à Deir el Médineh.* Cairo: Institut français d'Archéologie orientale.

Bryce, T. R. 1990. "The Death of Niphururiya and its Aftermath." *JEA* 76: 97–105.

——— 1998. *The Kingdom of the Hittites.* Oxford: Clarendon Press.

Cabrol, A. 1993. "Un socle de statue au nom de Séthi II." *Cahier de Recherches de l'Institut de Papyrologie et d'Égyptologie de Lille* 15: 31–35.

Callender, V. G. 2004. "Queen Tausret and the End of Dynasty 19." *SAK* 32: 81–104.

———— 2006. "The Cripple, the Queen & the Man from the North." 17/1: 48–63.

Caminos, R. 1955. "Two Stelae in the Kurnah Temple of Sethos I." In *Ägyptologische Studien*, edited by O. Firchow, 17–28. Berlin: Akademie-Verlag).

———— 1974. *The New Kingdom Temples of Buhen*, 2 vols. London: Egypt Exploration Society.

Cardon, P. 1979. "Amenmesse: An Egyptian Royal Head of the Nineteenth Dynasty in the Metropolitan Museum of Art." *MMJ* 14: 5–14.

Černý, J. 1929. "Papyrus Salt 124 (Brit. Mus. 10055)." *JEA* 15: 243–58.

———— 1952. *Paper and Books in Ancient Egypt*. London: H. K. Lewis & Co Ltd.

———— 1958. "A hieroglyphic ostracon in the Museum of Fine Arts at Boston." *JEA* 44: 23–25.

———— 1962. Review of Helck 1958, in *BiOr*19: 140–44.

———— 1965. "Egypt: from the Death of Ramesses III to the end of the Twenty-first Dynasty." In *Cambridge Ancient History*, 2nd ed., vol. 2, ch. xxxv. Cambridge: Cambridge University Press.

———— 1966. "A Note on the Chancellor Bay." *ZÄS* 93: 35–39.

Collier, M. 2004. *Dating Late XIXth Dynasty Ostraca*. Leiden: Nederlands Instituut voor het nabije Oosten.

Collier, M., A. Dodson and G. Hamernik 2010. "P. BM EA 10052, Anthony Harris, and Queen Tyti." *JEA* 96.

Creasman, P.P., W.R. Johnson, J.B. McClain and R.H. Wilkinson 2014. 'Foundation or completion? the status of Pharaoh-Queen Tausret's temple of millions of years'. *JNES* 77: 274–83.

Cruz-Uribe, E. 1977. "On the Wife of Merenptah." *GM* 24: 23–29.

———— 1978. "The Father of Ramses I: OI 11456." *JNES* 37: 237–44.

Daressy, G. 1900. "Remarques et notes." *RT* 22: 137–43.

———— 1909. *Cercueils des cachettes royales*. Cairo: Institut fran ais d'Archéologie orientale.

———— 1912. "Ramsès-Si-Ptah." *RT* 34: 39–52.

Davies, B. G. 1999. *Who's Who at Deir el-Medina. A Proposographic Study of the Royal Workmen's Community*. Leiden: Nederlands Instituut vor het Nibije Oosten.

Davis, T. M. et al. 1908. *The Tomb of Siptah; the Monkey Tomb and the Gold Tomb*. Westminster: Archibald Constable.

Dawson, W. R., E. P. Uphill and M. Bierbrier. 1995. *Who Was Who in Egyptology*. 3rd ed. London: Egypt Exploration Society.

De Meuleneare, H. 1968–72. "Le Vizir Ramesside Hori." *Annuaire de l'Institut de Philologie et d'Histoire orientales et slaves* 20: 191–96.

De Morgan, J., U. Bouriant, G. Legrain, G. Jéquier and A. Barsanti. 1894. *Catalogue des Monuments et Inscriptions de l'Egypte antique*, I/1. Vienna: Adolphe Holzhausen.

Delvaux, L. 1992. "Amenhotep, Horemheb et Paramessou: Les grandes statues de scribes à la fin de la 18e dynastie." In *L'atelier de l'orfèvre: mélanges offerts à Ph. Derchain*, edited by M. Broze and P. Talon, 47–53. Louvain: Peeters.

Desroches-Noblecourt, C. 1982. "Touy, Mère de Ramsès II, La Reine Tanedjmy et les Reliques de l'Expérience Amarnienne." In *L'Egyptologie en 1979: axes prioritaires de recherches*, II, 227–243. Paris: Centre National de la Recherche Scientifique.

Dodson, A. 1985. "The Tomb of King Amenmesse: Some Observations." *DE* 2: 7–11.

——— 1986a. "Was the sarcophagus of Ramesses III begun for Sethos II?" *JEA* 72: 196–98.

——— 1986b. "A note on the interior decoration of the coffer of the sarcophagus of Ramesses III, Louvre D1 = N337." *DE* 5: 35.

——— 1987. "The Takhats and some other Royal Ladies of the Ramesside Period." *JEA* 73: 224–29.

——— 1989. "Hatshepsut and 'her father' Mentuhotpe II." *JEA* 75: 224–26.

——— 1990a. "King Amenmesse at Riqqa." *GM* 117/118: 153–55.

——— 1990b. "Crown Prince Djhutmose and the Royal Sons of the Eighteenth Dynasty." *JEA* 76: 87–96.

——— 1992. "Death after Death in the Valley of the Kings." In *Death and Taxes in the Ancient Near East*, edited by S. Orel, 53–59. Lewiston: The Edwin Mellen Press.

——— 1994. *The Canopic Equipment of the Kings of Egypt*. London and New York: Kegan Paul International.

——— 1995. "Amenmesse in Kent, Liverpool and Thebes." *JEA* 81: 115–28.

——— 1997. "Messuy, Amada and Amenmesse." *JARCE* 34: 41–48.

——— 1999. "The Decorative Phases of the Tomb of Sethos II and their Historical Implications." *JEA* 85: 131–42.

——— 2000a. *After the Pyramids: the Valley of the Kings and Beyond*. London: Rubicon.

——— 2000b. "Towards a Minimum Chronology of the New Kingdom and Third Intermediate Period." *BES* 14: 7–18.

———— 2002. Review of Martin 1997. *JEA* 88: 270–71.

———— 2003. "The Burial of Members of the Royal Family During the Eighteenth Dynasty." In *Egyptology at the Dawn of the Twenty-First Century: Proceedings of the Eighth International Congress of Egyptologists, Cairo, 2000*, II, edited by Z. Hawass and L. P. Brock, 187–93. Cairo: The American University in Cairo Press.

———— 2004. "Bull Cults." In *Divine Creatures: animal mummies in ancient Egypt*, edited by S. Ikram, 72–105. Cairo: The American University in Cairo Press.

———— 2009a. *Amarna Sunset: Nefertiti, Tutankhamun, Ay, Horemheb and the Egyptian counter-reformation*. Cairo: The American University in Cairo Press.

———— 2009b. "On the alleged 'Amenhotep III/IV coregency' graffito at Meidum." *GM* 221: 25–28.

———— 2011. "Fade to Grey: The Chancellor Bay, *éminence grise* of the Late Nineteenth Dynasty." In *Ramesside Studies in Honour of K.A. Kitchen*, edited by M. Collier and S. Snape 145–58. Bolton: Rutherford Press.

———— 2012. *Afterglow of Empire: Egypt from the Fall of the New Kingdom to the Saite Renaissance*. Cairo: American University in Cairo Press.

Dodson, A. and D. Hilton. 2004. *The Complete Royal Families of Ancient Egypt*. London; New York: Thames and Hudson.

Dodson, A. and J. J. Janssen. 1989. "A Theban Tomb and its Tenants." *JEA* 75: 125–38.

Dodson, A. and S. Ikram. 2008. *The Tomb in Ancient Egypt*. London; New York: Thames and Hudson.

Dominicus, B. 2004. *Untersuchungen im Totentempel des Merenptah in Theben*, II: *Die Dekoration und Ausstattung des Tempels*. Mainz: Philipp von Zabern.

Dorman, P. F. 1988. *The Monuments of Senenmut: Problems in Historical Methodology*. London: Kegan Paul International.

Drenkhahn, R. 1980. *Die Elephantine-Stele des Sethnacht und ihr historischer Hintergrund*. Wiesbaden: Harrassowitz.

———— 1981. "Ein Nachtrag zu Tausret," *GM* 43: 19–22.

Drews, R. 1993. *The End of the Bronze Age: Changes in Warfare and the Catastrophe ca. 1200 B.C.* Princeton: Princeton University Press.

Dunham, D. and W. K. Simpson. 1974. *The Mastaba of Queen Mersyankh III. G 7530–7540*. Boston: Museum of Fine Arts, Department of Egyptian and Ancient Near Eastern Art.

Eaton-Krauss, M. 1981. "Seti-Merenptah als Kronprinz Merenptahs." *GM* 50: 15–21.

—— 1993. *The Sarcophagus in the Tomb of Tutankhamun*. Oxford: Griffith Institute.

Edgerton, W. F. 1933. *The Thutmosid Succession*. Chicago: University of Chicago Press.

Egberts, A. 1998. "Hard Times: The Chronology of 'The Report of Wenamun' Revised." *ZÄS* 125: 93–108.

Eisenlohr, A. 1872. "On the Political Condition of Egypt before the Reign of Ramses III." *TSBA* 1: 355–84.

El-Sawi, A. 1990. "A Limestone Statue of Sety II, from *jwn* - (Heliopolis)." *MDAIK* 46: 337–40.

Emery, W. B. 1935–38. "The order of succession at the close of the nineteenth dynasty." In *Mélanges Maspero*, I, 353–56. Cairo: Institut français d'Archéologie orientale.

Emery, W. B. and L. P. Kirwan. 1935. *The Excavations and the survey between Wadi es-Sebua and Adinidan 1929–1931*. Cairo: Government Press.

Engelbach, R. et al. 1915. *Riqqeh and Memphis VI*. London: British School of Archaeology in Egypt.

Epigraphic Survey 1940. *Medinet Habu, IV: Festival scenes of Ramses III*. Chicago; University of Chicago Press.

—— 1980. *The Tomb of Kheruef: Theban Tomb 192*. Chicago: Oriental Institute.

—— 1994, 1998. *Reliefs and Inscriptions at Luxor Temple*, I: *The Festival Procession of Opet in the Colonnade Hall*; II: *The Facade, Portals, Upper Register Scenes, Columns, Marginalia, and Statuary in the Colonnade Hall*. Chicago: Oriental Institute.

Ertman, E. 1993. "A First Report on the Preliminary Survey of Unexcavated KV10." *Kmt* 4/2: 38–46.

Fabretti, A., F. Rossi and R. V. Lanzone. 1888. *Regio Museo di Torino, Antichità egiziane*, II. Turin: Paravia.

Fazzini, R. A. 1972. "Some Egyptian Reliefs in Brooklyn." *Miscellanea Wilbouriana*, I: 33–70.

Fisher, M. M. 2001. *The Sons of Ramesses II*, 2 vols. Wiesbaden: Harrassowitz.

Forbes, D. C. 1998. "Another Ayrton/Davis Kings' Valley Discovery: The Gold Hoard of Queen Tausret & King Seti II." *Kmt* 9/2: 65–69.

Frandsen, P. J. 1991. "Editing reality: the Turin Strike Papyrus." In *Studies in Egyptology Presented to Miriam Lichtheim*, edited by S. Israelit-Groll, 166–199. Jerusalem: The Magnes Press.

Freu, J. 1988. "La tablette RS86.2230 et la phase finale du royaume d'Ugarit." *Syria* 65: 395–98.

Gaballa, G. A. 1977. *The Memphite Tomb-Chapel of Mose.* Warminster: Aris and Phillips.

Gaballa, G. A. and K. A. Kitchen. 1968. "Ramesside Varia I." *CdE* XLIII/86: 259–70.

Gabolde, L. 2005. *Monuments décorés en bas relief aux noms de Thoutmosis II et Hatchepsout à Karnak.* Cairo: Institut français d'Achéologie orientale.

Gardiner, A.H. 1912. "The Stele of Bilgai." *ZÄS* 50: 49–57.

———— 1932. *Late-Egyptian Stories.* Brussels: Fondation égyptologique Reine Élizabeth.

———— 1947. *Ancient Egyptian Onomastica,* 3 vols. Oxford: Oxford University Press.

———— 1953. "The Tomb of the General Haremhab." *JEA* 39: 3–12.

———— 1954. "The Tomb of Queen Twosre." *JEA* 40: 40–44.

———— 1958. "Only One King Siptah and Twosre not his wife." *JEA* 44: 12–22.

———— 1960. *The Kadesh Inscriptions of Ramesses II.* Oxford: Griffith Institute.

———— 1961. *Egypt of the Pharaohs.* Oxford: Oxford University Press.

Gatty, C. T. 1877. *Catalogue of the Mayer Collection,* I: *The Egyptian Antiquities.* Liverpool: Liverpool Free Public Library, Museum, and Gallery of Art.

Gauthier, H. 1914. *Le Livre des rois d'Égypte,* III. Cairo: Institut français d'Archéologie orientale.

Gitton, M. 1984. *Les divines épouses de la 18ᵉ dynastie.* Paris: Les Belles-Lettres.

Goedicke, H. 1975. *The Report of Wenamun.* Baltimore and London: The Johns Hopkins University Press.

———— 1979. "'Irsu, the Kharu' in Papyrus Harris." *WZKM* 71: 1–17.

———— 1981. "The "400-Year Stela" Reconsidered." *BES* 3: 25–42.

———— 1996. "Comments on the Sethnakhte Stela." *MDAIK* 52: 157–75.

Gomaà, F. 1973. *Chaemwese, Sohn Ramses' II. und Hohenpriester von Memphis.* Wiesbaden: Otto Harrassowitz.

Görg, M. 2000. "Mose—Name und Namensträger. Versuch einer historischen Annäherung." In *Mose. Ägypten und das Alte Testament,* edited by E. Otto, 17–42. Stuttgart: Verlag Katholisches Bibelwerk GmbH.

Grandet, P. 1993. *Ramsès III: histoire d'un règne.* Paris: Pygmalion/Gérard Watelet.

——— 2000. "L'exécution du chancelier Bay: O.IFAO 1864." *BIFAO* 100: 339–45.

——— 2003. *Catalogue des ostraca hiératiques non littéraires de Deîr el-Médînéh, IX: Nos 831–1000.* Cairo: Institut français d'Archéologie orientale.

——— 2005. *Le Papyrus Harris I (BM 9999)*, 2nd ed., 2 vols. Cairo: Institut français d'Archéologie orientale.

Gutgesell, M. 2002. *Die Datierung der Ostraka und Papyri aus Deir el Medineh, II: Die Ostraka der 19. Dynastie.* Hildesheim: Gerstenberg Verlag.

Gutgesell, M. and B. Schmitz. 1981. "Die Familie des Amenmesse." *SAK* 9: 133–41.

Habachi, L. 1957. "The Graffiti and Work of the Viceroys of Kush in the Region of Aswan." *Kush* 5: 13–36.

——— 1974. "Lids of the Outer Sarcophagi of Merytamen and Nefertari, Wives of Ramesses II." In *Festschrift zum 150 jährigen Bestehen der Berliner Ägyptologischen Museums, Staatliche Museen zu Berlin*, 105–12. Berlin: Akademie Verlag.

——— 1978. "King Amenmesse and the Viziers Amenmose and Kha'emtore: their Monuments and Place in History." *MDAIK* 34: 57–67.

——— 1980. "Königssohn von Kusch." *LÄ* III: 630–40.

——— 2001. *Tell el-Dab'a, I: Tell el-Dab'a and Qantir, the site and its connection with Avaris and Piramesse.* Vienna: Verlag der Österreichischen Akademie der Wissenschaften.

Hall, H. R. H. 1913. *Catalogue of Egyptian Scarabs, etc., in the British Museum, I: Royal Scarabs.* London: British Museum.

Hardwick, T. 2006. "The Golden Horus Name of Amenmesse?" *JEA* 92: 255–260.

Hassanein, F. 1985. "Le problème historique du Seth-her-khepshef, fils de Ramses III: à propos de la tombe n° 43 de la Vallée des Reines." *SAK Beiheft* 4: 63–66.

Hayes, W. C. 1935. *Royal Sarcophagi of the XVIII Dynasty.* Princeton, NJ: Princeton University Press.

——— 1959. *The Scepter of Egypt*, II. New York: Metropolitan Museum of Art.

Helck, W. 1955. "Zur Geschichte der 19. und 20. Dynastie." *ZDMG* 105: 39–52.

——— 1956. "Zwei thebanische Urkunden aus der Zeit Sethos' II." *ZÄS* 81: 82–87.

———— 1958. *Zur Verwaltung des Mittleren und Neuen Reichs.* Leiden/Cologne: E. J. Brill.

———— 1972. *Die Ritualdarstellung des Ramesseums*, I. Wiesbaden: Otto Harrassowitz.

———— 1990. "Drei Ramessidische Daten." *SAK* 17: 205–14.

———— 1995. "Die Datierung des Papyrus Greg." In *Gedenkschrift für Winfried Barta. ḥtp dj n ḥsj*, edited by D. Kessler and R. Schulz, 199–213. Frankfurt am Main: Peter Lang. Europäischer Verlag der Wissenschaften.

Hölscher, U. 1951. *The Excavation of Medinet Habu, IV: The Mortuary Temple of Rameses III*, II. Chicago: University of Chicago Press.

Hornung, E. 1990. *Valley of the Kings: Horizon of Eternity.* New York: Timken.

———— 2006. "The New Kingdom." In Hornung, Krauss and Warburton, eds. 2006, 197–217.

Hornung, E., R. Krauss and D.A. Warburton, eds. 2006. *Ancient Egyptian Chronology.* Leiden: Brill.

Ikram, S. 1989. "Domestic Shrines and the Cult of the Royal Family at El-'Amarna." *JEA* 75: 89–101.

Ikram, S. and A. Dodson. 1998. *The Mummy in Ancient Egypt: equipping the dead for eternity.* London and New York: Thames and Hudson.

Janssen, J. J. 1997. *Village Varia: ten studies on the history and administration of Deir el-Medina.* Leiden: Nederlands Instituut voor het Nabije Oosten.

Jaritz, H. 1992. "Der Totentempel des Merenptah in Qurna. 1. Grabungsbericht (1.–6. Kampagne)." *MDAIK* 48: 65–91.

———— 2001. "The Museum of the Mortuary Temple of Merenptah." *EgArch* 19: 20–24.

Jaritz, H., B. Dominicus and H. Sourouzian. 1995. "Der Totentempel des Merenptah in Qurna. 2. Grabungsbericht (7.und 8. Kampagne)." *MDAIK* 51: 57–83.

Jaritz, H., B. Dominicus, U. Minuth, W. Niederberger and A. Seiler. 1996. "Der Totentempel des Merenptah in Qurna. 3. Grabungsbericht (9. und 10. Kampagne)." *MDAIK* 52: 201–32.

Jaritz, H., B. Dominicus, W. Niederberger, H. Sourouzian and L. Stalder. 1999. "Der Totentempel des Merenptah in Qurna. 4. Grabungsbericht." *MDAIK* 55: 13–62.

Jaritz, H., M. Doll, B. Dominicus and W. Rutishauser. 2001. "Der Totentempel des Merenptah in Qurna. 5. Grabungsbericht." *MDAIK* 57: 141–70.

Jenni, H. (ed.) (in preparation.) *Das Grab Siptahs (KV 47) und das Grab der Königin Tiaa (KV 32).*

Johnson, K.L. and P.J. Brand 2013. "Prince Seti-Merenptah, Chancellor Bay, and the Bark Shrine of Seti II at Karnak." *JEH* 6: 19–45.

Jørgensen, M. 1998. *Catalogue Ny Carlsberg Glyptotek: Egypt II (1550–1080 B. C.)* Copenhagen: Ny Carlsberg Glyptotek.

Junge, F. 1987. *Elephantine,* XI: *Funde and Bauteile.* Mainz: Philipp von Zabern.

Kahl, J. 2007. *Ancient Asyut: The First Synthesis after 300 Years of Research.* Wiesbaden: Harrassowitz Verlag.

Kahn, D. 2010. "Who is Meddling in Egypt's Affairs? The Identity of the Asiatics in the Elphantine Stele of Sethnakhte and the Historicity of the Medinet Habu Asiatic War Reliefs." *Journal of Ancient Egyptian Interconnections* 2/1: 14–23.

Kampp. F. 1996. *Die thebanische Nekropole: zum Wandel des Grabgedankens von der XVIII. bis zur XX. Dynastie,* 2 vols. Mainz: Phillipp von Zabern.

Kitchen, K. A. 1968–90. *Ramesside Inscriptions: Historical and Biographical,* 8 vols. Oxford: Blackwell.

———— 1972. "Ramesses VII and the Twentieth Dynasty." *JEA* 58: 182–94.

———— 1982a. *Pharaoh Triumphant: the Life and Times of Ramesses II, King of Egypt.* Warminster: Aris and Phillips.

———— 1982b. "The Twentieth Dynasty Revisited." *JEA* 68: 116–25.

———— 1984. "Family Relationships of Ramesses IX and the Late Twentieth Dynasty." *SAK* 11: 127–34.

———— 1987. "Amenmesses in Northern Egypt." *GM* 99: 23–25.

———— 1990. "The Arrival of the Libyans in Late New Kingdom Egypt." In *Libya and Egypt, c 1300–750 BC,* edited by A. Leahy, 15– 27. London: University of London, School of Oriental and African Studies, Centre of Near and Middle Eastern Studies, and the Society for Libyan Studies.

———— 1993ff(a). *Ramesside inscriptions: translated and annotated. Translations.* Oxford: Blackwell.

———— 1993ff(b). *Ramesside inscriptions: translated and annotated. Notes and Comments.* Oxford: Blackwell.

———— 1994. "The physical text of Merenptah's Victory Hymn (the 'Israel Stela')." *JSSEA* 24: 71–77.

———— 1996. *The Third Intermediate Period in Egypt (1100–650 B.C.),* 3rd edition. Warminster: Aris and Phillips.

Klemm, R. 1988. "Vom Steinbruch zum Tempel. Beobachtungen zur Baus-
truktur einiger Felstempel der 18. und 19. Dynastie im ägyptischen
Mutterland." *ZÄS* 115: 41–51.

Korostovtsev, M. A. 1960. *путешествие Ун– Амуна в Библ.* Moscow:
Academy of Sciences.

Kozloff, A. 2004. "Amenhotep, King's Son of Kush: Did He Become
Amenhotep III?" *The 55th Annual Meeting of the American Research
Center in Egypt*, 62–63. Atlanta: American Research Center in Egypt.

Krauß, R. 1976. "Untersuchungen zu König Amenmesse (1. Teil)." *SAK* 4:
161–99.

———— 1977. "Untersuchungen zu König Amenmesse (2. Teil)." *SAK* 5: 131–74.

———— 1981. "Zur Historischen Einordnung Amenmesse und zur
Chronologie der 19/20 Dynastie." *GM* 45: 27–34.

———— 1997. "Untersuchungen zu König Amenmesse: Nachträge." *SAK*
24: 161–84.

———— 2000. *Moïse le pharaon.* Paris: Éditions du Rocher.

———— 2001. *Das Moses-Rätsel. Auf den Spuren einer biblischen Erfindung.*
Munich: Ullstein.

Krogman, W. M. and M. J. Baer. 1980. "Age at Death of Pharaohs of the
New Kingdom, Determined from X-Ray Films." In *An X-ray Atlas
of the Pharaohs*, edited by J. E. Harris and E. F. Wente, 188–212. Chicago: University of Chicago Press.

Lacau, P. 1906–25. *Statues et Statuettes des Rois et des Particuliers*, 3 vols.
Cairo: Institut fran ais d'Archéologie orientale.

Lauffray, J., R. Sa'ad and S. Sauneron. 1975. "Rapport sur les travaux de Karnak. Activités du Centre franco-égyptien en 1970–1972." In *Cahiers de
Karnak, V: 1970–1972*, edited by J. Lauffray, S. Sauneron and R. Sa'ad,
1–42. Cairo: Centre franco-égyptien d'f tude des Temples de Karnak.

Leblanc, C. 1988. "L'identification de la tombe de Henout-mi-Rê', fille
.de Ramsès II et grande épouse royale." *BIFAO* 88: 131–46.

———— 1989. *Ta Set Neferou: une necropole de Thebes-Ouest et son histoire*, I.
Cairo: Nubar Printing House.

Leclant, J. 1950. "Compte rendu des fouilles et travaux menés en f gypte
durant les campagnes 1948–1950." *Orientalia* 19: 360–73.

Leemans, C. 1841–82. *Monuments égyptiens du Musée d'Antiquités des Pays-
Bas ^ Leide.* Leiden: H. W. Hazenberg.

Lefébure, E. 1886–89. *Les hypogées royaux de Th bes.* Paris: Leroux.

Lefebvre, G. 1929a. *Histoire des grands pr tres d'Amon jusqu'a la XXIᵉ dynastie.* Paris: Geuthner.

——— 1929b. *Inscriptions concernant les grandes prêtres d'Amon Romê-Roy et Amenhotep*. Paris: Geuthner.

Lepsius, C. R. 1849–59. *Denkmaeler aus Aegypten und Aethiopien*, 6 vols. Berlin/Leipzig: Nicolaische Buchandlung.

——— 1897–1913, *Denkmaeler aus Aegypten und Aethiopien, Textband*, 5 vols. Leipzig: J. C. Hinrichs.

Lesko, L. H. 1966. "A Little More Evidence for the End of the Nineteenth Dynasty." *JARCE* 5: 29–32.

Loeben, C. 1987. "La porte sud-est de la salle-w3ḏt." In *Cahiers de Karnak*, VIII: *1982–85*: 207–223. Paris: Éditions Recherche sur les Civilisations.

MacGillivray, J. A. 2006. "A Jar from Sidon with the name of Pharaoh Tawosret." *Archaeology and History in Lebanon* 24: 121–28.

Mojsov, B. 1991/92. "A Royal Sarcophagus Reattributed." *BES* 11: 47–55.

Malek, J. 1999. *Topographical Bibliography of Ancient Egyptian Hieroglyphic Texts, Reliefs and Paintings*, VIII/1–2: *Objects of Provenance Unknown, Statues*. Oxford: Griffith Institute.

Manassa, C. 2003. *The Great Karnak Inscription of Merenptah: Grand Strategy in the 13th Century* BC. New Haven: Yale Egyptological Seminar.

Mariette, A. 1857. *Le Sérapeum de Memphis decouvert et décrit par Aug. Mariette. Ouvrage dédié à S. A. I. Mgr. le Prince Napoléon et publié sous les auspices de S. E. M. Achille Fould, ministre d'état*. Paris: Gide.

——— 1880a. *Abydos: description des fouilles exécutées sur l'emplacement de cette ville*, II. Paris: Imprimerie Nationale.

——— 1880b. *Catalogue général des monuments d'Abydos, découverts pendant les fouilles de cette ville*. Paris: Imprimerie Nationale.

Martin, G. T. 1989. *The Memphite Tomb of Ḥoremḥeb, Commander-in-Chief of Tut'ankhamūn*, I. London: Egypt Exploration Society.

——— 1997. *The Tomb of Tia and Tia. A Royal Monument of the Ramesside Period in the Memphite Necropolis*. London: Egypt Exploration Society.

Maspero, G. 1908. "King Siphtah and Queen Tauosrît." In *The Tomb of Siphtah; the Monkey Tomb and the Gold Tomb*, by T. M. Davis, xiii–xxix. Westminster: Archibald Constable.

[Mayer, J.] 1852. *Egyptian Museum, No. VIII, Colquitt-Street, Liverpool*. Liverpool: Mawdsley and Son.

McCarthy, H.L. 2008. "Rules of decorum and expressions of gender fluidity in Tawosret's tomb." In *Sex and Gender in Ancient Egypt*, edited by C. Graves-Brown, 83-113. Swansea: The Classical Press of Wales.

Molleson, T. and M. Cox. 1993. *The Spitalfields Project, II: The Anthropology, the Middling Sort.* York: Council for British Archaeology.

Mond, R. and O. Myers. 1940. *The Temples of Armant.* London: Egypt Exploration Society.

Montet, P. 1951. *La nécropole royale de Tanis, II: Les constructions et le tombeau de Psousennes à Tanis.* Paris.

Morales, A. J. 2001. "The Suppression of the High Priest Amenhotep: a Suggestion to the Role of Panhesi." *GM* 181: 59–75.

Murnane, W. J. 1990. *The Road to Kadesh: a Historical Interpretation of the Battle Reliefs of King Sety I at Karnak,* 2nd edition. Chicago: Oriental Institute.

Naville, E. 1910. *The XIth Dynasty Temple at Deir el-Bahari, II.* London: Egypt Exploration Fund.

Naville, E. and F. L. Griffith. 1890. *The Mound of the Jew* and *The Antiquities of Tell el Yahûdiyeh.* London: Egypt Exploration Fund.

O'Connor, D. 1991. "Mirror of the cosmos: the palace of Merenptah." In *Fragments of a Shattered Visage: the Proceedings of the International Symposium of Ramesses the Great,* edited by E. Bleiberg, R. E. Freed and A. K. Walker, 167–198. Memphis, TN: Memphis State University.

——— 2000. "The Sea Peoples and the Egyptian Sources." In Oren (ed.) 2000: 85–102.

Oren, E. D. (ed.). 2000. *The Sea Peoples and Their World: a reassessment.* Philadelphia: University of Pennsylvania, The University Museum.

Osing, J. 1979. "Zur Geschiche der späten 19. Dynastie." *SAK* 7: 252–71.

Parkinson, R. 1997. *The Tale of Sinuhe and Other Ancient Egyptian Poems.* Oxford: Oxford University Press.

——— 1999. *Cracking Codes: the Rosetta Stone and Decipherment.* London: British Museum Press.

Peden, A. J. 1994a. *The Reign of Ramesses IV.* Warminster: Aris and Phillips.

——— 1994b. "A Note on the Accession Date of Merenptah." *GM* 140: 69.

Peet, T. E. 1930. *The Great Tomb-Robberies of the Twentieth Egyptian dynasty: being a critical study, with translations and commentaries, of the papyri in which these are recorded.* Oxford: Clarendon Press.

Petrie, W. M. F. 1897. *Six Temples at Thebes 1896.* London: Methuen.

——— 1917. *Scarabs and Cylinders with names.* London: British School of Archaeology in Egypt/Egyptian Research Account.

——— 1925a. *A History of Egypt, III,* 3rd edition. London: Methuen.

———— 1925b. *Buttons and Design Scarabs*. London: British School of Archaeology in Egypt.

Petrie, W. M. F. et al. 1888. *Tanis* II, *Nabesha (Am) and Defenneh (Tahpanhes)*. London: Egypt Exploration Fund.

Piacentini, P. and C. Orsenigo. 2004. *La Valle dei Re Riscoperta: i giornali scavo di Victor Loret (1898–1899) e altri inediti*. Milan: Università degli Studi di Milano/Skira.

Pillet, M. 1922. "Rapport sur les traveaux de Karnak." *ASAE* 22: 235–60.

Porter, B. and R.B. Moss. 1960–64; 1972; 1974–81; 1934; 1937; 1939; 1952. *Topographical Bibliography of Ancient Egyptian Hieroglyphic Texts, Reliefs and Paintings*, I: *The Theban Necropolis*, 2nd ed.; II, *Theban Temples*, 2nd ed; III, *Memphis*, 2nd edition by J. Málek; IV: *Lower and Middle Egypt*; V: *Upper Egypt: Sites*; VI: *Upper Egypt: Chief Temples (excl. Thebes)*; VII: *Nubia, Deserts, and Outside Egypt*. Oxford: Clarendon Press/Griffith Institute.

Posener, G. 1977. "La complainte de l'échanson Bay." In *Fragen an die altägyptische Literatur: Studien zum Gedenken an Eberhard Otto*, edited by J. Assmann, E. Feucht and R. Grieshammer, 385–97. Wiesbaden: Dr. Ludwig Reichert Verlag.

Prisse d'Avennes, A. 1847. "Antiquités égyptiennes du Musée britannique (British Museum)." *Revue Archeologique* III: 693–723.

Pusch, E. B. 1999. "Tausret und Sethos II in der Ramses-Stadt." *Ägypten und Levante* IX: 101–109.

Quibell, J. E. 1898. *The Ramesseum*. London: Quaritch.

Quirke, S. 2004. *Egyptian Literature 1800 BC: Questions and Readings*. London: Golden House Publications.

Redford, D. B. 1986a. *Pharaonic King-Lists, Annals and Day-Books*. Mississauga: Benben Books.

———— 1986b. "The Ashkelon Relief at Karnak and the Israel Stela." *IEJ* 36: 188–200.

———— 1992. *Egypt, Canaan, and Israel in Ancient Times*. Princeton: Princeton University Press.

Redford, S. 2002. *The Harem Conspiracy. The Murder of Ramesses III*. DeKalb, IL: Northern Illinois University Press.

Reeve, J. and M. Adams. 1993. *The Spitalfields Project*, I: *the Archaeology, Across the Styx*. York: Council for British Archaeology.

Reeves, C. N. 1990a. *Valley of the Kings: The decline of a royal necropolis*. London: Kegan Paul International.

——— 1990b. *The Complete Tutankhamun: the King, the Tomb, the Royal Treasure*. London: Thames and Hudson.

Robins, G. 1981. "The Value of the Estimated Ages of the Royal Mummies at Death as Historical Evidence." *GM* 45: 63–68.

Romer, J. 1974. "Tuthmosis I and the Bibân el-Molûk: Some Chronological Considerations." *JEA* 60: 119–33.

Rougé, E. De 1858. *Étude sur une stèle égyptienne, appartenant à la Bibliothèque impériale*. Paris: Imprimarie Impériale.

Ruffle, J. and K. A. Kitchen. 1979. "The family of Urhiya and Yupa, High Stewards of the Ramesseum." In *Glimpses of Ancient Egypt: Studies in Honour of H. W. Fairman*, edited by J. Ruffle, G. A. Gaballa and K. A. Kitchen, 55–74. Warminster: Aris and Phillips.

Ryan, D. P. 1992. "Some observations concerning uninscribed tombs in the Valley of the Kings." In *After Tut'ankhamūn*, edited by C. N. Reeves, 21–27. London and New York: Kegan Paul International.

Sa'ad, R. 1975. "Fragments d'un monument de Toutânkamon retrouvés dans le IXe pylône de Karnak." In *Cahiers de Karnak, V: 1970–1972*, edited by J. Lauffray, S. Sauneron and R. Sa'ad, 93–109. Cairo.

Sams, J. 1839. *Ancient Egypt: Objects of Antiquity forming part of the Extensive & rich collections from Ancient Egypt, brought to England by, or now in the possession of J. Sams*. London: Executed for & under the immediate inspection of the Proprietor.

Schaden, O. J. 1993. "Amenmesse Project Report." *NARCE* 163: 1–9.

——— 1994. "Some Observations on the Tomb of Amenmesse (KV10)." In *Essays in Egyptology in Honor of Hans Goedicke*, edited by B. Bryan and D. Lorton, 243–54. San Antonio: Van Siclen Books.

——— 2004. "KV-10: Amenmesse 2000." *ASAE* 78: 129–49.

Schaden, O. J. and E. Ertman. 1998. "The Tomb of Amenmesse (KV10): The First Season." *ASAE* 73: 116–155.

Schiff Giorgini, M. 1965, 1998–2003. *Soleb*, I, III–V. Florence: Sansoni/Cairo: Institut fran ais d'Archéologie orientale.

Schmidt, H. C. 1994. "Ein Fall von Amtsanmassung? Die Gottesgemahlin Nefertari-Meritenmut." *GM* 140: 81–92.

Schmidt, H. C. and J. Willeitner. 1997. *Nefertari, Gemahlin Ramses' II*. Mainz: Philipp von Zabern.

Schneider, T. 2003. "Siptah und Beja: Neubeurteilung einer historischen Konstellation." *ZÄS* 130: 134–46.

——— 2011. "Conjectures about Amenmesse: Historical, Biographical, Chronological." In *Ramesside Studies in Honour of K. A.*

Kitchen, edited by M. Collier and S. Snape 445–51, Bolton: Rutherford Press.

Schulman, A. R. 1986. "The Royal Butler Ramesses-sami'on." *CdE* 61/122: 187–202.

Smith, G. E. 1912, *The Royal Mummies*. London: Constable.

Smith, H. S. 1976. *The Fortress of Buhen*, II: *The Inscriptions*. London: Egypt Exploration Society.

Sourouzian, H. 1988. "Henout-mi-Rê, fille de Ramses II et grande épouse du roi." *ASAE* 69: 365–71.

——— 1989. *Les Monuments du roi Merenptah*. Mainz: Philipp von Zabern.

Spalinger, A. 1982. Review of Drenkhahn 1980, *BiOr* 39: 272–88.

Spencer, P. A. 1997. *Amara West*, I. London: Egypt Exploration Society.

——— (ed.) 2007. *The Egypt Exploration Society—the early years*. London: Egypt Exploration Society.

Steindorff, G. 1936. "Skarabäen mit Namen von Privatpersonen der Zeit des Mittleren und Neuen Reichs aus der Sammlung S. M. des Königs Fuâd I." *ASAE* 36: 161–86.

——— 1937. *Aniba*, II. Glückstadt: Augustin.

Strouhal, E. 1982. "Queen Mutnodjmet at Memphis: anthropological and paleopathological evidence." *L'Égyptologie en 1979: axes prioritaires de recherches*, II, 317–22. Paris: Éditions du Centre national de la Recherche scientifique.

Thiem, A.-C. 2000. *Speos von Gebel es-Silsileh. Analyse der architektonischen und ikonographischen Konzeption im Rahmen des politischen und legitimatorischen Programmes der Nachamarnazeit*, 2. Wiesbaden: Harrassowitz.

Thijs, A. 1998. "Reconsidering the End of the Twentieth Dynasty, part I: The fisherman Pnekhtemope and the date of BM 10054." *GM* 167: 95–108.

——— 1999a. "Reconsidering the End of the Twentieth Dynasty, partII," *GM* 170: 83–100.

——— 1999b. "Reconsidering the End of the Twentieth Dynasty, part III: Some Hitherto Unrecognised Documents from the *wḥm mswt*." *GM* 173: 175–92.

——— 2000a. "Reconsidering the End of the Twentieth Dynasty, part IV: The Harshire-family as a Test for the Shorter Chronology." *GM* 175: 99–104.

———— 2000b. "Reconsidering the End of the Twentieth Dynasty, part V: P. Ambras as an Advocate of a Shorter Chronology." *GM* 179: 69–84.

———— 2001a. "Reconsidering the End of the Twentieth Dynasty, part VI: Some Minor Adjustments and Observations Concerning the Chronology of the Last Ramessides and the *wḥm-mswt*." *GM* 181: 95–103.

———— 2001b. "Reconsidering the End of the Twentieth Dynasty, part VII. The History of the Viziers and the Politics of Menmare," *GM* 184: 65–73.

———— 2003. "The troubled careers of Amenhotep and Panehsy: The High Priest of Amun and the Viceroy of Kush under the last Ramessides." *SAK* 31: 289–306.

———— 2004a. "Pap. Turin 2018, the journeys of the scribe Dhutmose and the career of the Chief Workman Bekenmut." *GM* 199: 79–88.

———— 2004b. "'My father was buried during your reign': the burial of the High Priest Ramessesnakht under Ramses XI." *DE* 60: 87–95.

Thomas, E. 1966. *Royal Necropoleis of Thebes*. Princeton: privately printed.

Tosi, M. and A. Roccati. 1972. *Stele e altri epigrafi di Deir el Medina*. Turin: Edizioni d'Arte Fratelli Pozzo.

Uphill, E. P. 1984. *The temples of Per Ramesses*. Warminster: Aris and Phillips.

Valbelle, D. 1985. *«Les ouvriers de la tomb»: Deir el-Médineh à l'époque Ramesside*. Cairo: Institut français d'Archéologie orientale.

Vandier, J. 1971. "Ramsès-Siptah." *RdE* 23: 165–91.

von Beckerath, J. 1951. *Tanis und Theben. Historische Grundlagen der Ramessidenzeit in Ägypten*. Glückstadt: J. J. Augustin.

———— 1956. "Die Reihenfolge der letzten Köninge der 19. Dynastie." *ZDMG* 106: 241–51.

———— 1962. "Queen Twosre as Guardian of Siptah." *JEA* 48: 70–74.

———— 1994. *Chronologie des ägyptischen Neuen Reiches*. Hildesheim: Gerstenberg.

———— 1999. *Handbuch der ägyptischen Königsnamen*, 2nd edition. Mainz: Philipp von Zabern.

———— 2000. "Bemerkungen zur Chronologie der Grabräuberpapyri." *ZÄS* 127: 111–16.

———— 2001. "Überlegungen zum Zeitabstand zwischen Ramses II. und dem Ende der XXI. Dynastie." *GM* 181: 15–18.

Waddell, W. G. 1940. *Manetho*. Cambridge, MA: Harvard University Press/London: William Heinemann.

Weeks, K. R. (ed.). 2000. *Atlas of the Valley of the Kings.* Cairo: The American University in Cairo Press.

Wente, E. F. 1966. "The Suppression of the High Priest Amenhotep." *JNES* 25: 73–87.

———— 1980. "Age at Death of Pharaohs of the New kingdom, Determined from Historical Sources." In *An X-ray Atlas of the Pharaohs*, edited by J. E. Harris and E. F. Wente, 234–85. Chicago: University of Chicago Press.

Wente, E. F. and J. E. Harris. 1992. "Royal Mummies of the Eighteenth Dynasty: a biologic and Egyptological approach." In *After Tut'ankhamūn*, edited by C. N. Reeves, 2–20. London and New York: Kegan Paul International.

Wilkinson, R. H. 2012. "The "Temple of Millions of Years" of Tausret'. In *Tausret: forgotten queen and pharaoh of Egypt*, edited by R.H. Wikinson, 67–91. New York: Oxford University Press.

Wilkinson, R. H. (ed.) 2011. *The Temple of Tausret: the University of Arizona Egyptian Expedition Tausret Temple Project, 2004-2011.* [Tucson, AZ]: University of Arizona Egyptian Expedition.

Yurco, F. J. 1979. "Amenmesse: Six Statues at Karnak." *MMJ* 14: 15–31.

———— 1986. "Merenptah's Canaanite Campaign." *JARCE* 23: 189–215.

———— 1990. "3,200-Year-Old Picture of Israelites Found in Egypt." *BAR* 16/5: 20–38.

———— 1997. "Was Amenmesse the Viceroy of Kush, Messuwy?" *JARCE* 34: 49–56.

Yurco, F. 1978. "Merenptah's Palestinian Campaign." *JSSEA* 8: 70.

INDEX

Names of kings are CAPITALIZED.
For the use of numbers and letters to distinguish homonyms, *see* Dodson
and Hilton 2004.

Generalissimo (*iry-r mš⁽ wr*) 31
Gezer 18
God's Father Beloved of the God
(*it-nṯr mrw-nṯr*) 11
Gurob (Miwer) 74, 79

Harmaïs (legendary king of Egypt)
67
Harris I, Papyrus *see* London,
British Museum
BM EA9999
HATSHEPSUT 32, 95, 96, 97,
134
Hatti *see* Hittite Empire
Hattusilish III (king of the Hittites)
158
Heir (*iw⁽*) 11
Heliopolis 19, 23, 79, 86, 102, 117,
124
Henutmire (wife of Rameses II) 7,
8, 9, 144, 145
Herakleopolis *see* Ihnasiya
Hermopolis *see* Ashmunein
high priest of Amun at Karnak (*ḥm
nṯr tpy n 'Imn*) 37, 104, 122,
130, 131, 154
high priest of Ptah, at Memphis
(*wr ḥrp ḥmwt*) 9, 23, 72, 75,
104, 117
Hittite Empire 2, 10, 11, 12, 17,
18, 128
HOREMHEB 1, 2, 14, 22, 39, 40,
89, 94, 121, 129, 134, 143,
151
Hori A (high priest at Memphis)
23, 72, 75
Hori I (son of Khaemwaset C,
vizier) 23, 72, 75, 85, 104,
124
Hori II (First Charioteer; viceroy
of Nubia) 104, 124, 159
Hori III (First Charioteer; viceroy)
105
Hori IV (high priest of Amun at
Karnak) 104

Horus 13, 26, 47, 48, 50, 52, 55,
57, 69, 85, 93, 105, 112,
115, 122, 138, 145, 152
Huy (Chief Craftsman of the Lord
of the Two Lands) 74
Huy (Chief of Madjay, Overseer of
Works) 23

Ihnasiya (Herakleopolis) 19
Ipy (First Charioteer, son of
Nayiba) 105
Irsu 90, 91, 97, 120, 121, 122, 158
Iset A (wife of Thutmose II) 144
Iset C (daughter of Amenhotep III)
8
Iset D (QV51; wife of Rameses III
and mother of Rameses VI)
152, 153
Isetneferet A (wife of Rameses II) 7
Isetneferet B (daughter of Rameses
II) 13
Isetneferet C (wife of Merenptah)
13, 14, 145
Isetneferet D (daughter of
Merenptah) 14
Isis 50, 57, 59, 61, 75, 97, 102,
128
Israel 18, 146, 166
Israel Stela (Cairo CG34025) 18,
19, 20, 146
Iyroy (high priest of Ptah at
Memphis) 104, 117

Josephus (Jewish historian) 67, 154
jubilee (*ḥb-sd*) 5, 11, 65

Karnak
Ashkelon Wall 12, 17
Cour de la Cachette 12, 16, 17,
18, 20, 76
East Temple of Amun-Re-
Harakhty 55
Festival Hall 52, 53, 55, 56